Statecraft and Diplomacy
in the Twentieth Century

LIVERPOOL HISTORICAL STUDIES
published for the
Department of History, University of Liverpool

P. M. H. BELL

Statecraft and Diplomacy in the Twentieth Century

Essays presented to P. M. H. Bell

edited by
DAVID DUTTON

Published for the
Department of History
University of Liverpool

LIVERPOOL UNIVERSITY PRESS
1995

Liverpool Historical Studies, no. 13
General Editor: C. H. Clough

First published 1995
by Liverpool University Press
Senate House, Abercromby Square, Liverpool, L69 3BX

British Library Cataloguing in Publication Data
A British Library CIP record is available
ISBN 0-85323-379-9

Printed in the European Union by
Antony Rowe Limited, Chippenham, England

Contents

Preface

This book has been a collaborative venture in more senses than that implied by its format as a collection of essays written by eight different scholars. I am pleased to acknowledge here the help which I have received in its preparation.

It was Professor Peter Hennock's excellent idea that I should organise a colloquium in honour of Philip Bell. Ralph White offered invaluable assistance in arranging this event. On the day of the colloquium itself Cecil Clough, as General Editor of the series *Liverpool Historical Studies*, suggested that I should turn the venture into a book. I am grateful for his continuing support and that of his fellow members of the Publications Committee of the Department of History at the University of Liverpool. As a self-confessed computer-illiterate my own role in the preparation of the volume for publication is best described as that of an awe-inspired spectator. Mrs. Alison Bagnall typed the entire work with an enviable combination of speed and expertise. Professor Paul Hair has given generously of his time, with help from Jon Lawrence, to transform a typescript into camera-ready copy. Their skills command my admiration and demand my thanks. Robin Bloxsidge of the Liverpool University Press has been, as ever, the model of an efficient and helpful publisher. Without the contributors, of course, there could be no book and I must thank all of them for their collaboration and cooperation in producing the individual chapters. Their enthusiasm for their task was no doubt largely a function of the high regard they all feel for Philip Bell. To him this book is presented with a combination of professional respect and warm personal friendship.

David Dutton
Liverpool, November 1994

Contributors

Martyn Cornick, of the Department of European Studies at Loughborough University, is articles editor of the quarterly journal *Modern and Contemporary France*. He has published widely on French intellectual history and Anglo-French relations, and is researching aspects of reciprocal perceptions in France and Britain.

David Dutton is Senior Lecturer in Modern History at the University of Liverpool. He is the author of *Simon: a Political Biography of Sir John Simon* (1992) and *His Majesty's Loyal Opposition: the Unionist Party in Opposition 1905-15* (1992).

M.R.D. Foot was an army officer from 1939 to 1945; worked with the SAS Brigade during 1944; returned to Oxford; spent six years as Professor of Modern History at the University of Manchester, 1967-1973; and has written *inter alia* on Gladstone, on resistance and on SOE in France.

Christine Giuliani teaches French at the University of Liverpool. She is currently preparing an edition of her grandfather's 1914-1918 trench diary.

Alan Sharp is Professor of International Studies at Magee College, the Londonderry campus of the University of Ulster. His book, *The Versailles Settlement: Peacemaking in Paris 1919*, was published in 1991.

Philip M. Taylor is Reader in International Communications and Deputy Director of the Institute of Communications Studies at the University of Leeds. He is also Executive Secretary of the Inter-University History Film Consortium and associate editor of the *Historical Journal of Film, Radio and Television*. His most recent book is *War and the Media: Propaganda and Persuasion in the Gulf War*, published in 1992.

Geoffrey Warner was educated at the Universities of Cambridge and Paris. He has worked at the Royal Institute of International Affairs and taught at the Universities of Reading, Hull and Leicester before becoming Professor of European Humanities at the Open University. He is the author of *Pierre Laval and the Eclipse of France* (1968), *Iraq and Syria, 1941* (1979), and of numerous articles on twentieth-century international history.

Ralph White is Senior Fellow in the Department of Politics and Contemporary History at the University of Salford. He edited, with S.F. Hawes, *Resistance in Europe, 1939-1945* (1975) and is the author of articles and papers on Europeanism during the inter-war period.

Abbreviations

ANP	Archives Nationales, Paris
AP	Avon Papers, University of Birmingham Library
BL	British Library
BN	Bibilothèque Nationale, Paris
CID	Committee of Imperial Defence
CUL	Cambridge University Library
HLRO	House of Lords Record Office
HMSO	Her Majesty's Stationery Office
IUHFC	Inter-University History Film Consortium
LC	Library of Congress, Washington D.C.
LHCMA	Liddell Hart Centre for Military Archives, King's College, London
MAE	Ministère des Affaires Etrangères, Paris
PRO	Public Record Office, London
	CAB Cabinet papers
	FO Foreign Office papers
RL	Franklin Delano Roosevelt Library, Hyde Park, New York
DBFP	E.L. Woodward, R. Butler et al., *Documents on British Foreign Policy, 1919-1939, First Series* (27 vols, London, 1947-1986)
DBFP1A	W.N. Medlicott et al., *Documents on British Foreign Policy, 1919-1939, Series 1A* (7 vols, London, 1966-1975)
FRUS	*Foreign Relations of the United States* (Washington, 1870 et seq.)
HJFRT	*The Historical Journal of Film, Radio and Television*

Introduction

At the end of September 1993 Philip Bell retired after thirty-six years on the staff of the University of Liverpool. Four months earlier friends and colleagues had gathered for a one-day symposium held in his honour. The present volume is based upon that event.

A Yorkshireman by birth – with all the best of the qualities which that geographical derivation implies – Philip Bell graduated from Wadham College, Oxford, with First Class Honours before doing postgraduate research under F.W. Deakin at St. Antony's. Happily, it was at Oxford that he met his future wife, Marjorie. His first appointment was as Assistant Lecturer in History at Aberdeen University; but he moved to the then Department of Modern History at Liverpool in 1957, the first appointment of Professor David Quinn. He watched the department expand through the sixties and seventies before it fused with its Medieval sister into the new Department of History, and he retired as Reader in that Department.

His first book dealt with the question of disestablishment in Wales and Ireland, but for most of the last quarter century the primary focus of his research interest has been on the diplomatic history of the twentieth century and, in particular, on the twin and often inter-related themes of Anglo-French relations and the diplomacy of the Second World War. These themes have determined the shape of both the colloquium and this book.

Philip's second book was entitled *A Certain Eventuality*, a study of British policy at the time of the fall of France in 1940. Though twenty years old now, this book has lasted extraordinarily well and still figures prominently in any well constructed bibliography on the traumatic events of 1940. His *Origins of the Second World War in Europe*, published in 1986, is rightly regarded as a minor masterpiece. It is not only a superb textbook for which many generations of undergraduates will have cause to be grateful, it is also a stimulating essay which the specialist will read with profit, causing even the best informed of scholars to think again about the received wisdom on this enormously important subject. In a footnote to his recent Prothero Lecture Professor Sir Michael Howard wrote: 'It was only some months after completing the text of this lecture that I came across the treatment of the 'Thirty Year War' question by Mr. P.M.H. Bell in his excellent work *The Origins of the Second World War in Europe*. I am deeply ashamed of this oversight. Had I read Mr. Bell's work, I would have adopted a different approach, if indeed I had tackled the problem at all.'[1]

Most recently, Philip has published *John Bull and the Bear*, a study of British propaganda and the Soviet Union during the Second World War. In this innovative book we see the author's consummate skill in charting new ground in a significant area of research. One reviewer enthused: 'To have a senior historian and veteran of the Public Record Office such as Philip Bell plunge into the records of British public opinion and propaganda ... is a sheer delight. The result is an important book, a rare example of how to fuse effectively diplomatic documents with the archives of mass communication.'[2] His current project – an ambitious study of the whole field of Anglo-French relations in the twentieth century – is now nearing completion and eagerly awaited. It will arrive at a timely moment, ninety years after the signing of the *Entente Cordiale*. These books have, of course, been liberally interspersed with a host of important chapters, articles, conference papers and historical films. In sum it amounts to a major research output which has deservedly won him high regard both in Britain and abroad, especially in France. All Philip's work is characterised by an enviable clarity and the ability to focus on the key issues within any historical topic with insight, but without pretension, and with a meticulous regard for the historical record.

It is also fair to add that while the Department of History at Liverpool has boasted a fine scholar, it was also fortunate to have an excellent and much appreciated teacher, who never had much difficulty in instilling his own enthusiasm for history into the minds of countless undergraduates. Year in and year out, Philip's second year course on twentieth-century international history was among the most popular in the Department, guaranteeing a full house for his final year Special Subject classes. Perhaps to his own disadvantage Philip is also possessed of a logical and reliable administrative brain, of which both the Department and the Faculty made good use.

* * *

The essays in this volume are arranged, as far as possible, in chronological order. Five are based on papers given at the colloquium mentioned above; the remaining three have been specially contributed. Martyn Cornick's wide-ranging piece on the myth of 'Perfidious Albion' provides an appropriate starting point. It seeks to go beyond the confines of conventional diplomatic history as the author lucidly takes the reader through many centuries of Anglo-French misunderstanding. It is an approach which will appeal to Philip Bell himself, who for several years collaborated with the Department of French at Liverpool University in an imaginative teaching programme which used literary texts as historical source material.[3] David Dutton's chapter looks at Anglo-French relations in the Balkan Campaign of World War One, an expedition whose soldiers came to look upon themselves as the forgotten army of that war. (Indeed the editor might be permitted to note that in his own incisive survey of the Great War Philip Bell failed to list this campaign among the principal theatres of operations!)[4] Even as allies in a military campaign the relations of Britain and France were paralysed by mutual suspicion and recrimination. Little had changed by the time that the fighting ceased, as Alan Sharp demonstrates in his analysis of Anglo-French relations in the wake of the Treaty of Versailles. The two countries which proclaimed to share a common commitment to democracy soon got themselves 'in a tangle' once more.

If Philip would permit his attitudes and beliefs to be summed up by shorthand labels, he would certainly accept the description of 'francophile' and would probably have no great difficulty with 'Eurosceptic'. He would not see any incompatibility between the two. His association with France over many years has imbued him with a warm regard for that country, its people and its culture. But his work as an historian has given him a profound respect for the nation-state as the single most powerful force in diplomatic relations. So he would no doubt have shared much of the scepticism of the British Foreign Office at the Briand Plan of 1930, that early and tentative blue-print for European integration explored by Ralph White in his chapter, 'Through a glass, darkly'. The ambivalence of the Anglo-French association is reflected in Christine Giuliani's contribution on the relationship between Anthony Eden and Charles de Gaulle. As British politicians in World War Two took time off from their struggle against Germany to ponder the role which postwar France, probably led by de Gaulle, might play in a British-dominated Western Europe, few could have imagined that within a generation their successors would have become supplicants for membership of a European community dominated by Germany and France, the latter country still headed by de Gaulle. Perhaps the Anglo-French relationship is seen at its best at a level below that of high politics in the era of the French Resistance, a topic authoritatively surveyed in this volume by M.R.D. Foot, who was himself awarded the *Croix de Guerre* for services with the resistance in Brittany.

The remaining essays touch upon other themes related to Philip Bell's research. In conjunction with Ralph White he has produced two compilation films for the Inter-University History Film Consortium. Philip M. Taylor looks at the use made of film in Britain as a propaganda weapon during the Second World War, and the stages by which its potential as a contribution to ultimate victory was slowly appreciated. Finally, Geoffrey Warner attempts to penetrate the mind of Franklin D. Roosevelt to elucidate the thinking of the American President on the sort of postwar world he was seeking to secure. That vision had considerable implications for Great Britain. The country's relations with continental Europe were always going to be in part determined by the priority accorded to the Special Relationship with the United States, and much of Philip Bell's work on the Second World War has an American dimension to it. Professor Warner reminds us that Anglo-American relations during the war were never as uncomplicated and harmonious as the Churchillian legend once led us to believe. Had Roosevelt's ideas on the postwar world been better known, it is hard to believe that they would have been entirely welcome to his British allies.

Notes

1. M. Howard, 'A Thirty Years' War? The Two World Wars in Historical Perspective', *Transactions of the Royal Historical Society*, sixth series, vol.3 (1993) p.171.
2. Philip M. Taylor, in *History*, 253 (1993) pp.342-3.
3. See P.M.H. Bell and S. Sykes, 'Novel and history in twentieth-century France', ibid., 212 (1979) pp.391-5.
4. P.M.H. Bell, 'The Great War and its Impact', in P. Hayes (ed.), *Themes in Modern European History 1890-1945* (London and New York, 1992) pp.132-3.

The myth of 'perfidious Albion' and French national identity

Martyn Cornick

This contribution is an exploration of some considerations relating to French anglophobia and definitions of French national identity, arising from a paper given at a conference on 'French views of Britain' held at the British Institute in Paris. That paper examined in some detail the repercussions of a notorious attack on Britain published by Henri Béraud in 1935, entitled *Faut-il réduire l'Angleterre en esclavage?*[1] In the immediate short term this attack gave rise to a diplomatic protest, while in the longer term it contributed towards a general deterioration in Anglo-French relations to the extent that French public opinion regarding Britain and British policy toward its neighbour never truly recovered before the Fall of France in June 1940. After this, under the influence of Laval and others in the Vichy hierarchy, Britain was transmuted back into the hereditary enemy that it always had been, at least down to the *Entente Cordiale* of 1904. This, certainly, was what Vichy- and German-inspired collaborationist propaganda told the French people from July 1940 onwards. The myth of 'perfidious Albion' was enthusiastically revived in a wide range of propaganda efforts. The questions approached here are the following: what is the nature of this myth, what are its origins, how was it sustained, and how can it be explained?

* * *

French anglophobia is a feature which has, relatively speaking, not received extensive critical or historical attention in the same way that French anti-Semitism has. Like anti-Semitism, it is a complex phenomenon that may be studied on different levels. To begin with, it may be considered simply as the manifestation, or result, of 'problems of communication', as the French economic historian François Crouzet demonstrates in an important article.[2] Indeed, on one level, historic anglophobia may be characterized as a latent force deeply ingrained in the French national unconscious which, periodically, has blazed up again when fed by the oxygen of international rivalry or tension. However, in view of renewed debates on the nature of *national identity,* it should also be interpreted as a rather more complex phenomenon. In common with other varieties of xenophobia, anglophobia is an integral part of nationalism; in the case of France, it is part of the history of a reductionist ideology that excludes, by definition, everything that is not French.[3] Also by definition, Identity excludes the Other, whatever its origin – 'l'Angleterre, c'est l'anti-Français', to put it most simplistically.[4] Thus, viewed in this perspective, it is part of the history of French national identity, or how French national identity came variously to be defined. In other words, national identity may be defined not only according to *intrinsic* characteristics, for example in the way that Fernand Braudel defines it; instead it may also be defined according to the *extrinsic* characteristics of other, especially rival, peoples and nations.[5] The concern of this chapter is, therefore, to examine the extent to which anglophobia has in the past been a determining component of French national identity, a component whose durability continues to invoke references to the echoing myth of 'perfidious Albion'.[6]

This myth is deeply implanted in the French collective unconscious. To borrow an expression from Philip Bell, it forms part of the 'mental baggage' of the French. Indeed, the usefulness of the notion 'mental baggage' has been acknowledged by the French historian Jean-Louis Crémieux-Brilhac. In the introduction to his authoritative work on France during the 'Phoney War', Crémieux-Brilhac explains:

> La notion de *bagage mental*, à laquelle l'historien anglais Philip Bell et moi sommes attachés, est ici capitale. Le passé mental commande toujours notre présent, il le détermine plus que jamais dans une période où l'accélération de l'histoire a été si forte. ... Non seulement, chacun évoque à tout moment des situations anciennes et des stéréotypes familiers ... mais il semble que dans beaucoup d'esprits l'imprévu des événements réactive des strates psychologiques et des attitudes mentales antérieures, dans une oscillation qui accroît encore la mobilité de l'opinion habituelle en temps de crise: d'où une grande instabilité des jugements et des humeurs.[7]

So, when Henri Béraud, for example, unleashed his attack on Britain in 1935, he immediately struck a chord with the French public. It sufficed to reiterate the phrase 'perfide Albion' and compile a catalogue of historical examples of perfidy, and proceed to make them relevant to the contemporary situation: by doing so, and in accord with the process identified above by Crémieux-Brilhac, he was immediately understood by the public. His views were thus calqued on a common reference point, and as such were understood even by those who did not necessarily share his political views, or those of his newspaper, *Gringoire*.[8] The 'mental baggage' referred to here is the stuff of myth and prejudice, of *idées fixes*, or of crude national stereotypes that reached their greatest and most enduring potency at the end of the last century.[9] Put another way, this contribution will suggest some ways in which this 'mental baggage' was filled and left on the threshold of the twentieth century.

For the sake of convenience the nature of this 'mental baggage' will be examined in terms of three central, sometimes interlocking, factors which, indeed, may also be considered as fields for further research:

    1. the foundations of national identity/nationalist ideology;

    2. the images of the English as disseminated in major reference works and in popular literature;

    3. the influence of racist ideology based on pseudo-scientific ideas.

* * *

Although the intention is to focus primarily on the period following the French Revolution, it is important to note none the less that England and the Anglo-Saxons were generally viewed as France's foremost hereditary enemies ever since the Norman period. In a fascinating study investigating the image of Britain in medieval French literature, Peter Rickard demonstrates that English perfidy, or treachery, had become such a byword by the fifteenth century that a popular saying could ironize: 'Dieu nous gard ... / De la loyauté d'un Anglois'. And hundreds of years of accumulated testimony persuaded the French that:

> the English cannot be trusted to observe a truce: they negotiate cynically, fully intending to break their word when it is expedient to do so. ... Their record is of unredeemed insincerity, treachery and perjury, for which God will eventually punish them; they have never been known to keep their word and they never will.[10]

A Burgundian chronicler even suggested that this character trait was a 'heritage from their Saxon ancestors who ... conquered England by treachery'. One could expect no more from a people who were supposed to have tails, who drank too much, who could not speak French properly and who, in short, were devilish in character.[11]

There is a 'political' linkage here with the Trojan myth as it contributed to medieval constructions of French identity. Colette Beaune demonstrates that in medieval Europe, 'les origines troyennes de la nation et de la dynastie sont évoquées partout. Toute histoire nationale commence par le récit de la migration des princes troyens.' Between 1300 and 1500 the Trojan myth was manipulated to serve internal French politics in conjunction with the Hundred Years' War. As is the case with so many myths, there are heroes and traitors among the protagonists. Drawing on a pioneering article by A. Bossuat on the use of Trojan origin myths in medieval France, Beaune shows how negative elements from these played an anti-English role.[12] According to such ideas, the treacherous Antenor was the ancestor of the English, whilst Brutus, himself a direct descendant of Troy, migrated to found Brittany, whence his descendants also settled in Britain. Beaune continues:

> De toute façon, ces Troyens bretons ne dominent plus aujourd'hui l'Angleterre, car des Saxons barbares germaniques ont envahi l'île [i.e., before 1300] les tuant tous 'en grand crudélité'. Les rescapés se sont enfuis en petite Bretagne. Les Anglais ne peuvent donc se glorifier des exploits de Brutus ou d'Arthur. Il ne sont qu'une race mêlée, capables de toutes les mauvaises actions.[13]

The intention here is not, however, to give a catalogue of examples of anti-English feeling from the Middle Ages onwards. The important point is that 'the French nation was, above all, forged and tempered in the great struggle known as the Hundred Years' War'.[14] After all, this great struggle bequeathed to posterity the figure of Joan of Arc as the most enduring emblem from what came to be treated as an enemy occupation of France, and as such could conveniently be resurrected at various times throughout history (including the time of the Boer War and Second World War), to stoke up nationalism and revive anti-British feeling.[15] Furthermore, Christopher Allmand has noted an anglophobe tradition in French historical writings on the late medieval period, particularly those of the nineteenth century dealing with the Anglo-French conflict.[16]

*   *   *

Today the Revolution is recognized as the 'official' founding event of the modern French nation state.[17] The 1988 presidential election campaign and the 1989 bicentenary festival showed clearly that the modern French Republic traces its origins to the Revolution and First Republic. Political festivals in France are, of course, nothing new. Mona Ozouf is one among many historians who have demonstrated how the revolutionaries and their propagandists, including Mercier and David, celebrated the Revolution as it unfolded: festivals, theatre, painting, versifiers, actors and poets all contributed to an enormous and unprecedented propaganda effort designed to carry the people with them.[18] Yet it is rarely acknowledged, to take just a few examples from a substantial output of verse inspired by celebrating the Revolution, that one can find plenty of evidence to support the view that anglophobia was adopted as a definitional theme of French, Jacobin-influenced, national identity during the 1790s.

This early, revolutionary, French Republic clearly identified the English as the people most responsible for co-ordinating the counter-revolution: they were tyrants, they were oppressors, they sheltered and financed *émigrés* and intriguers such as the Comte d'Antraigues.[19] The revolutionaries inherited the 'perfidious Albion' myth from their monarchist predecessors and enthusiastically adopted the English as their own hereditary enemies. A work published in 1821, which gathers together a remarkable collection of texts dating from the 1780s up to 1820, provides numerous examples of patriotic hymns and anthems recited or sung during the many revolutionary festivals.[20] In October 1793, Augustin, Comte de Ximénez (1776-1817) published a poem celebrating the fact that France, as part of an historical process dating back to the republics of ancient Greece and Rome, had at last reached 'the republican era'. The first three lines from the climactic final stanza of this ode were even adapted for use on a republican calendar:

Attaquons dans ses eaux, la perfide Albion!
Que nos fastes s'ouvrant par sa destruction
Marquent les jours de la victoire!

Que le monde vers nous, lentement attiré,
Sente de quels fardeaux nous l'aurons délivré,
Et nous pardonne notre gloire.[21]

Another versifier, Lebrun, published an *impromptu* on learning that the English had declared war on France:

Eh bien! la Liberté sera toute française!
Complice des tyrans, complice de ses fers,
En s'armant contre nous, la nation anglaise
Se trahit elle-même et trahit l'Univers.[22]

The fourth stanza of Rouget de Lisle's 'Hymne des Marseillais', the first battle hymn of the French Republic, contains the line 'Tremblez tyrans! et vous perfides', where the epithet 'perfides' leaves no doubt as to the object of the inference.[23] Marie-Joseph Chénier, younger brother of the more celebrated poet André Chénier, produced many patriotic hymns and odes which were performed at various *Fêtes de la Fédération* throughout the 1790s.[24] When the French recaptured Toulon from English forces in 1793, Chénier composed a hymn which was sung to the crowd at the Festival held on the Champ de Mars to celebrate this victory. The hymn begins:

Toulon redevenu Français
N'étend plus ses regards sur une onde captive;
Son roc purifié par nos justes succès
Menace Albion fugitive.[25]

Chénier's themes and examples were simple: the French would defeat this 'insolent' and 'tyrannical' rival whenever and wherever they came into conflict because France had 'Virtue' and 'Right' on her side. Even Nature favoured the Republic:

Les feux qu'ont allumé des ennemis pervers,
Dirigés contre eux-mêmes, ont foudroyé leurs têtes;
Et leurs vaisseaux, tyrans des mers,
Sont poursuivis par les tempêtes.

French naval forces would carry the message of equality to English shores, and perhaps one day 'Liberty would shine over the sombre Thames':

Anglais! vos serviles vaisseaux
Teints du sang qui coula sous les remparts de Gênes,
D'une cité française osant souiller les eaux,

Venaient nous apporter des chaînes.
Les nôtres à Plimouth [sic] portant l'égalité,
Consoleront la Manche à des brigands soumise,
Et le jour de la liberté
Luira sur la sombre Tamise.

In a comparison employed very frequently in the history of anglophobia, just as the young Roman republic had done before, the whole Universe would rise up to destroy Britain, the new Carthage:

En vain vous prétendez encor
Appésantir sur l'onde un trident tyrannique;
Rois, ministres guerriers, vainqueurs avec de l'or,
Triomphans par la foi punique,
L'Univers se soulève; il remet en nos mains
Le soin de recouvrer le public héritage,
Et les bras des nouveaux Romains
Renverseront l'autre Carthage.

In another philippic, 'Le Chant des victoires, hymne de guerre', Chénier mythologized even minor events to symbolize the heroic nature of the revolutionary struggle, such as the attack by three British vessels on the outnumbered French ship, symbolically named *Le Vengeur*:

Avare et perfide Angleterre,
La mer gémit sous tes vaisseaux;
Tes voiles pèsent sur les eaux,
Tes forfaits pèsent sur la terre. ...
Lève-toi, sors des mers profondes,
Cadavre fumant du *Vengeur!*
Toi qui vit le Français vainqueur
Des Anglais, des feux et des ondes.
D'où partent les cris déchirans?
Quelles sont les voix magnanimes?
Les voix des braves expirans,
Qui chantent du fond des abîmes.[26]

The anti-British theme extended even to comic verse: the following rhyming couplets were recited at the theatre of the Opéra-Comique National in the rue Favart, Paris:

Descendons dans nos souterrains!
La Liberté nous y convie;
Elle parle, républicains,
Et c'est la voix de la patrie!
Lavez la terre en un tonneau,
En faisant évaporer l'eau,
Bientôt le nitre va paraître;
Pour visiter Pitt en bateau,
Il ne nous faut que du Salpêtre.[27]

By year VI of the revolutionary era these attacks and their themes had become commonplace. Thus in 1798 a citizen Désorguès penned a hundred-line song entitled 'Chant de guerre contre l'Angleterre'. Using the familiar analogy with ancient Rome, the battle-hymn began:

Quand la paix, de la Seine embellit le rivage,
Quel appareil guerrier vient frapper nos regards?
Rome a-t-elle juré la perte de Carthage,
Et dans ses coupables remparts
Veut-elle de ses droits venger l'antique outrage?
Oui; qu'Albion tremble pour ses foyers!
Némésis a sonné l'heure de la vengeance.[28]

This poem ranges over many examples of English perfidy and tyranny, but concentrates notably on the maritime theme, and ends by urging on the Revolution's young warriors in their secular struggle to free Europe and the world from this ubiquitous oppressor:

J'ai juré de frapper un peuple audacieux,
Et du fond de ces noirs abîmes,
Un long cri de vengeance est monté jusqu'aux ciëux
Aux rives de la Seine il retentit encore.
Volez, jeunes guerriers, à de nouveaux succès!
Arrachez mon trident superbes Anglais!
Allez, le monde vous implore;
Rendez-lui le bonheur, le commerce et la paix!

Napoleon's propagandists continued in much the same vein: the official song written to celebrate the Emperor's coronation was printed and distributed to the crowds by order of the police. It contained the refrain:

En bravant de l'Anglais l'impuissante fureur,
Chantez Napoléon! chantez votre empéreur![29]
Thus Jacobin and Napoleonic poets, borrowing their imagery from previous, classical rivalries between Rome and Carthage, and writing in unalloyed support of their political masters, inherited and perpetuated the image of England as hereditary enemy.

* * *

The foregoing images of 'perfidious Albion' and the English were already the stuff of literature, even if they had a practical, or propaganda, function; they were composed by writers who had not necessarily been to Britain, and who certainly did not need to care that they were not presenting a true picture. This second category examines examples of how, in the mid-nineteenth to early twentieth centuries – an age that witnessed the gradual spread of mass-literacy and the rise of mass participation in politics – anglophobia continued as a negative determinant of French identity.[30] Here we shall turn to the Larousse *Grand Dictionnaire Universel* and to late nineteenth-century French adventure fiction.

The *Grand Dictionnaire Universel* was published by Pierre Larousse in instalments from the early 1860s onwards. This huge edifice, despite the modesty of its preface, certainly deserves to be placed in the tradition of d'Alembert's great Enlightenment *Encyclopédie*.[31] It incorporates entries on 'Albion', 'Anglais', as well as a very long essay on 'Angleterre'.[32] Under 'Albion', the expression 'perfidious Albion' is explained thus:

Ce mot [Albion] se retrouve principalement dans cette locution très populaire chez nous: *la perfide Albion*, qui sert à caractériser la mauvaise foi, la perfidie traditionnelle [sic] du gouvernement anglais. Cette expression, d'abord poétique, est devenue en quelque sorte triviale, et personne n'oserait aujourd'hui l'employer sérieusement. C'est le *Punica fides* des Romains. Toutefois, il est bon d'ajouter qu'il n'y a pas entre les deux locutions une similitude complète; que l'expression française a plus de vérité que l'expression latine [sic].[33]

Under the substantives 'Anglais' and 'Anglaise', the dictionary's compilers

gathered together many extracts from a wide range of French literary
sources, including Beyle, Dumas, Balzac and, of course, Hippolyte Taine:
L'ANGLAIS est devenu, de tous les hommes, le plus capable
d'agir utilement et puissamment dans toutes les voies, le travailleur
le plus productif et le plus efficace, comme son boeuf est devenu
la meilleure bête à viande, son mouton la meilleure bête à laine,
et son cheval le meilleur coureur.[34]
The compilers also drew readers' attention to one or two special uses of the
word 'Anglais', the most interesting of which is the familiar expression
meaning 'créancier dur, impitoyable', as illustrated by this extract from Henri
Murger: 'Baptiste, s'il vient des ANGLAIS pour moi, vous direz que je suis
dans les Basses-Pyrénées'. This 'ancient' use of the term is traced by the
dictionary back to the time of the English occupation of France:
[Les Anglais], s'étant emparés de tout l'argent du pays, prêtaient
aux habitants aux conditions les plus rigoureuses. ... Quant à nous,
nous croyons que c'est une allusion à cette prétention singulière de
nos voisins, qui, de tous temps, se sont considérés comme nos
créanciers, réclamant tantôt la Guyenne, tantôt la Normandie ...
jusqu'à ce que vînt Jeanne Darc [sic] qui leur a prouvé que nous
ne leur devions rien du tout.
In addition, a number of anecdotes are included which illustrate a notion of
the English character that is entirely preconceived. The compilers write:
On connaît la réputation d'excentricité, d'originalité et d'égoïsme
national dont jouissent chez nous les Anglais. Ce sont ces divers
côtés du caractère britannique que les petites anecdotes suivantes
sont destinées à mettre en relief.
Two of these anecdotes are as follows:
Milord Hervey, voyageant dans l'Italie et se trouvant non loin
de la mer, traversa une lagune dans l'eau de laquelle il trempa son
doigt. 'Ah! ah!' dit-il, 'l'eau est salée, ceci est à nous.'
Un Anglais passant par Blois, descendit dans une auberge dont
l'hôtesse était rousse et très-revêche. En partant, il écrivit sur son
album: 'Toutes les femmes de Blois sont rousses et acariâtres.'[35]
Most interesting of all, however, is the section of text included at the end
of the very long entry 'Angleterre'. After covering a broad range of topics

– history and geography, architecture and religion, and so on – it ends with a section entitled 'L'Angleterre jugée par Jacques Bonhomme'. This section, purporting to weigh up *anglomanie* and *anglophobie* in France, deploys grammatical and rhetorical structures which lead the reader to anticipate a dialogue; it is, however, a virtually undisguised torrent of anglophobia. For two complete, closely printed pages (covering eight columns of the dictionary) Jacques Bonhomme, 'affligé d'une incurable anglophobie ... puisée dans l'étude de l'histoire',[36] unashamedly berates John Bull, compiling as he goes a catalogue of evidence intended to demolish the view held by French *anglomanes* that England should be revered as a haven of liberal democracy and model society. The diatribe opens innocently enough with a sketch of the natural features and climatic influences which have blessed and shaped the English national character (Taine's ideas are very much to the fore here; his predominance is further examined below):

> Un vaste réseau de voies navigables; un sol qui regorge de fer et de houille, masses énormes de matériaux offerts par la nature à l'industrie de l'homme; un climat triste et brumeux qui semble prescrire l'action, interdire l'oisiveté, sous peine d'énervement moral et de *spleen*; des côtes découpées en sinuosités innombrables et qui offrent d'admirables facilités au dévelopment de la marine; un territoire limité, enserré par l'Océan, dont les vastes solitudes ont toujours sollicité les hommes aux expéditions lointaines, aux grandes aventures de la mer: telles sont, avec les énergies de ton caractère national, les causes principales qui ont concouru au dévelopment de ta puissance maritime, et surexcité ton activité commerciale et cet esprit exclusivement mercantile, passe-moi ce mot, qui est un des traits distinctifs de ta race.[37]

These are the features which have helped to lay the foundations of the greatest colonial empire in the world. But there follows a brusque change of tone in mid-paragraph:

> Mais toi, et c'est ici que tu vas trouver quelques arêtes dans le poisson, toi, pauvre John, vile multitude industrielle et agricole, tu n'en es pas moins l'un des peuples les plus misérables de la terre; en dépit de ton travail obstiné, tu languis dans la misère et l'abjection.

This leads to a veritable catalogue of miseries, miseries inflicted in particular on the people of Ireland, on the agricultural population, and on the inhabitants of the largest cities. In a short digression on the indescribable poverty of London, 'Jacques Bonhomme' generalizes axiomatically:

> Dans aucun pays la bataille de la vie n'est plus âpre et plus obstinée, la défaite plus tragique. Quiconque fléchit tombe écrasé. Dans ta société d'airain, nulle pitié pour le faible, pour l'inhabile ou l'imprévoyant. La pauvreté est méprisée comme le serait un vice ou une mauvaise action.[38]

What were the causes of this deplorable exploitation? The greedy aristocracy were the primary cause, having concentrated and usurped economic and political power in a constitutionalized oligarchy. The effect of this state of affairs was to stifle progress, to prevent the physical and moral emancipation of the lower classes.

Comparing military organization in the two countries, 'Jacques Bonhomme' affirms that every Frenchman would willingly shed his own blood for his country since he owes his existence to the *patrie*, whereas each time the British needed to fight, the government had recourse to 'despotic measures' such as press-gangs. After criticisms of the corruptibility of the whole system, the paragraph ends in a threatening vision:

> Quant à tes soldats, tout le monde connaît le tarif de leur courage: ils n'avancent qu'en grognant si le gin est de médiocre qualité et si le roastbeef n'est pas cuit à point. Un jour, mes zouaves escaladeront tes côtes, et, par dessus le marché, ta tour de Londres, l'estomac vide et en sabots, comme leurs anciens de Sambre-et-Meuse.[39]

Jacques Bonhomme's most acid comments were reserved for what he conceived to be Britain's rôle on the international stage. All over the world and throughout history, 'John Bull' had fomented internal divisions and encouraged betrayals within nations in order to dominate them:

> Cette étonnante infatuation de la légitimité de ta domination sur tous les points de l'univers est même un trait particulier à ta race [sic]. Le monde est ton domaine, l'Océan t'appartient, les peuples sont tes ennemis quand ils se refusent à être tes humbles auxiliaires. Partout où l'un des tiens pose le pied, partout où il

peut puiser une goutte d'eau salée dans le creux de sa main, il se sent chez lui, et il dit: 'Ceci est à moi.'[40] And 'Bonhomme' identifies a symbol in the natural, maritime world to represent this rôle, a symbol which was quickly taken up thereafter by numerous illustrators and polemicists: this is 'le poulpe', or, the octopus:

> Ses tentacules, armes terribles dont tout son corps est recouvert, ont l'effrayante propriété de faire le vide partout où ils touchent. Le malheureux qui tombe au milieu de cet engrenage ... est à l'instant étouffé et dévoré. Eh bien, l'Angleterre est ce poulpe, et ses mille tentacules enserrent et sucent le monde.

Napoleon, 'ce Prométhée moderne', was right to characterize the British as a 'nation of shopkeepers', for he recognized only too well that they would stop at nothing to satisfy their lust for world markets. In short, selfishness, or egotism, was the most important determining British characteristic:

> Le vice radical de ta race, ton égoïsme, tant national qu'individuel, explique à la fois ta tendance à l'envahissement et à l'exclusion, à l'accaparement des richesses et à l'isolement. Tu ne t'associes jamais avec une autre race, ni par les intérêts, ni par les idées. ... Ta politique est ici d'accord avec ton tempérament national, car tu n'as nulle préoccupation d'associer et de civiliser, mais de posséder et d'exploiter.[41]

After dismissing the *Entente Cordiale* (the first one, that of the 1840s) as an 'oeuvre d'art', this cascade of anglophobia ends in apocalyptic mode, to underscore the fundamental opposition of the two nations, fixed as they were in two separate and irreconcilable identities:

> Il est hors de doute qu'on verrait les haines de race, les rivalités séculaires ... se réveiller avec une violence qui étonnerait cet âge d'indifférence et de scepticisme. ... En l'état actuel des choses et avec un adversaire aussi puissant que toi, il s'agirait cette fois d'un duel à mort qui partagerait l'univers en deux camps, comme la lutte d'Athènes et de Sparte, comme celle de Rome et de Carthage; et qu'on verrait en présence non-seulement deux intérêts, mais encore deux races, deux principes, et en quelque sorte deux civilisations.[42]

In a work that alludes in the preface to the fact that it is a scientific, encyclopaedic dictionary in the Enlightenment tradition, this section confirms, and even consecrates, the existence of a 'perfidious Albion' myth to which nationalists could and did turn in future.

* * *

Twentieth-century anglophobes, such as Henri Béraud or Louis-Ferdinand Céline, lived their formative years in an age in which *feuilletons* and pulp adventure stories were a prime source of adolescent distraction. The fiction of Jules Verne, for instance, is full of stereotypical, 'cardboard cut-out' characters.[43] We shall turn our attention to three examples of this *Boy's Own Paper* type fiction for evidence of how England and the English were portrayed. All three works were best sellers and went through several editions, and all three conceive of England as 'perfidious Albion'.

The first is Alfred Assolant's *Aventures merveilleuses, mais authentiques, du Capitaine Corcoran*. According to the Bibliothèque Nationale catalogue this work, first published in 1867 – the time of Larousse's dictionary – went through seven reimpressions between 1872 and 1898.[44] It appeared in Hachette's 'Bibliothèque rose illustrée' series for 'children and adolescents'. It is a paradigm of such adventure fiction. Set in 1856, it relates the exploits of a handsome 25-years-young sea captain and his tame tigress, Luison. Responding to a challenge set by the Lyon Academy, Corcoran sets off to India to appropriate a valuable Hindu book (called the 'Gouroukaramta') that has, so far, eluded the grasp of the Indians' colonizers. Apart from the amusement it affords, this rather surreal work is useful for its portrayal of the English, especially considering the image it was to hold up to French teenagers over the last thirty years of the nineteenth century. Captain Corcoran is himself stereotypical: he is a Breton mariner, and as such has a natural antipathy to the British that can be traced back to his medieval antecedents.[45] When he finally meets the sympathetic Indian prince of the story, the 'Holkar', the reader is treated to Corcoran's description of Franco-British rivalry:

> Seigneur, il y a dans ce vaste univers deux espèces d'hommes, ou,
> si vous le voulez, deux races principales – sans compter la vôtre
> – c'est le Français et l'Anglais, qui sont l'un à l'autre ce que le

dogue est au loup, ce que le tigre est au buffle, ce que la panthère est au serpent à sonnettes. Ce sont deux races affamées, l'une de louanges, l'autre d'argent, mais toutes deux également batailleuses et prêtes à se mêler des affaires d'autrui. J'appartiens à la première de ces deux races.[46]

Unsurprisingly, Corcoran prevails over the wily British, and ends the first volume honoured by the Indians as a Maharajah. In the second part, the British deploy their secret weapon in the shape of George William Doubleface [sic!], who is none other than the chief of the British secret police in Calcutta. Only by resorting to typical treachery can the British restore advantage; but what is interesting here is the use of the figure of the secret agent. In the twentieth century the British Intelligence Service becomes an endlessly recurrent theme of anglophobia; in this work it is in use already. The book ends in the spirit of 'if you can't beat them, join them', as Corcoran finally becomes an ally of Queen Victoria, with a pension of 25 million rupees, due mainly to the 'natural cowardice of the Hindus'.[47] The latter are portrayed, simplistically, as an inferior race, unworthy of the heroism of their potential liberators, and the reader is left in little doubt about how easily they had been cowed by their treacherous colonizers.[48]

The second example is *Le Sergent Simplet à travers les colonies françaises* by the pseudonymous Paul d'Ivoi.[49] This book recounts the picaresque adventures of two *sous-officiers*, Claude Bérard and Marcel Dalvan. They meet on a train at Grenoble station and abscond in search of adventure, fleeing first to England via Etaples and Hastings. From there they take a circuitous route by train to Liverpool, where they embark for the United States with a young lady with the promising name of Miss Diana Gold-Pretty. Again, the formulaic plot takes them to India. Yet the exoticism they might have been expecting is tempered by the appalling misery in which the British deliberately keep the native population. 'Comment les 250 millions d'Hindous n'ont-ils pas le courage d'exterminer les cent mille Anglais qui détiennent la fortune de l'Inde?', asks one of the French characters.[50] In the native's answer to this crucial question, once again the ideological charge of anglophobia is foregrounded, and today one can ponder the impact it would have had on its young readers:

La force des Anglais provient uniquement de la faiblesse de leurs sujets. Ceci m'amène tout naturellement à une comparaison. En France, naïfs comme vous l'êtes, vous déclarez à tout propos et hors de propos, que les Saxons vous sont supérieurs en fait de colonisation. Les colonies françaises deviennent *français*: voyez le Canada, la Louisiane, l'Algérie, la Guadeloupe, la Réunion. Les colonies anglaises ne subissent aucune assimilation. Pourquoi? Parce que vous entreprenez la *conquête morale* des peuples, tandis que les habitants de la Grande-Bretagne cherchent seulement à les *confisquer commercialement*.[51]

Mahrattes, the educated Indian interlocutor of this encounter, is clearly imbued with Jacobin principles, and looks forward to the time when his people will be liberated: 'Les jours de liberté viendront, quand les pavillons tricolores franchiront les portes de l'Occident.'[52] Thus young French readers learned that the French colonial empire was relatively humane, compared to the unspeakable brutality 'typical' of British colonies. In every port-of-call in their frenetic world tour, one message is clear: the British are cynical oppressors who do not hesitate to vent their spleen against the French themselves. At one point, during a pause in Siam, where the French and British nearly came to blows in 1893, it is stated aphoristically that 'se moquer du petit Français paraît délectable à tout citoyen du Royaume-Uni'.[53] The supposed 'superiority complex' of the British, and the corresponding 'inferiority complex' of the French, although they were nothing new, provoked a great deal of debate during the last decade of the nineteenth century.[54]

The third example of this pervasive anglophobia is the work by another pseudonymous author, Captain Danrit, *Guerre maritime et sous-marine*.[55] A first version of this work had been published in 1902 under the title *La Guerre fatale, France-Angleterre*.[56] This appeared before the *Entente Cordiale* of April 1904; yet a revised and corrected version was published in a cheap edition in fifteen volumes in 1908, after the *Entente*. Just as significant is that this introductory volume was sold at the exceptionally low price of 50 centimes in order to bring 'these enthralling adventures to the widest possible public'. The novel is shot through with a violent hatred of the English, and is very reminiscent of the sort of diatribes penned later during the 1930s by Henri Béraud. Henri d'Argonne, another Breton mariner, has his hatred of the English reinforced when he falls in love with Maud Carthy, a young Irish woman. The Irish question provided a rich seam for anglophobes, and their union in this novel is undoubtedly intended to be symbolic. D'Argonne's anti-English feeling is expressed in many passages throughout this book, and the following extract is typical:

> Généreux et loyal, [D'Argonne] haïssait l'Angleterre pour ses violences et ses brutalités; il la détestait par nature, spontanément, parce qu'il avait en lui le culte du beau et du bien et que partout où il avait recontré l'Anglais, il s'était heurté au génie du mensonge et du mal. D'ailleurs, cette antipathie profonde, Henri d'Argonne n'était pas le seul à l'éprouver. *En France, elle s'est généralisée dans la masse, malgré la pression officielle et la duperie de l'entente cordiale.*[57] [emphasis added]

Here narration turns to diatribe, and the undiluted anglophobia of the Commander runs on for several paragraphs, and recurs at several points throughout the rest of the work.

These three examples are not isolated: they spawned many parallels or imitations, such as Louis Boussenard's *Capitaine Casse-Cou*, a novel about a young Frenchman who went off to seek adventure against the British in the Boer War, an action probably inspired by the real-life French Colonel Villebois de Mareuil, who led the Legion of Foreign Volunteers in the Transvaal against the British, and who perished there under British fire.[58]

* * *

The anglophobic element in definitions of French national identity derived essentially from (and should be considered in the context of) a central trend in nineteenth-century thought. As historians such as Leon Poliakov and Eugen Weber have pointed out, and as we saw in Jacques Bonhomme's dictionary diatribe described above, the search for historical foundations upon which to base contemporary and evolving concepts of national identity drew on notions of racial difference.[59] Racist ideas, whose vocabulary derived originally from linguistic taxonomies, sought to divide Europe into Anglo-Saxons, Gauls and Latins, Aryans and Semites, and were dressed up as pseudo-science by thinkers such as the Comte de Gobineau.[60] Throughout the later two-thirds

of the nineteenth century it is possible to trace the development of such
thinking, from the work of the historian Augustin Thierry through to the
work of Hippolyte Taine, whose books on English literature and whose
account of his journeys to Britain were perennially influential.[61]

Taine's overarching theory, expounded in the introduction to his *Histoire
de la littérature anglaise*, was based upon *race, milieu,* and *moment*. A great
admirer of English civilization, and by no means an anglophobe, Taine chose
to study English literature precisely because it best suited his methodology:
it presented itself as a convenient, self-contained object for study whose
different identity would, none the less, be thrown into stark relief when
submitted to the scrutiny of the French historical analyst:

> J'ai choisi l'Angleterre, parce qu'étant vivante encore et soumise
> à l'observation directe, elle peut être mieux étudiée qu'une
> civilisation détruite dont nous n'avons plus que les lambeaux, et
> parce qu'étant différente, elle présente mieux que la France des
> caractères tranchés aux yeux d'un Français.[62]

Taine's work on English literature and his affinities for the culture, politics
and social system of the English have been studied[63]. For the present
discussion, suffice it to note that his description of the early Saxons, based
on his favoured blend of *race, milieu* and *moment*, predetermined his
conception of contemporary English national character:

> De grands corps blancs, flegmatiques, avec des yeux bleus
> farouches, et des cheveux d'un blond rougeâtre; des estomacs
> voraces, repus de viande et de fromage, réchauffés par des
> liqueurs fortes; un tempérament froid, tardif pour l'amour, le goût
> du foyer domestique, le penchant à l'ivrognerie brutale:*ce sont là
> encore aujourd'hui les traits que l'hérédité et le climat
> maintiennent dans la race,* et ce sont ceux que les historiens
> romains lui découvrent d'abord dans son premier pays. ...
> Ajoutez-y le plaisir de se battre. *Ce n'est pas avec de tels instincts
> qu'on atteint vite à la culture; pour la trouver naturelle et
> prompte, il faut aller la chercher dans les sobres et vives
> populations du Midi.* Ici [in England] le tempérament lent et lourd
> reste longtemps enseveli dans la vie brutale; au premier aspect,
> *nous autres, gens de race latine, nous ne voyons jamais chez eux*

que de grandes et grosses bêtes, maladroites et ridicules quand elles ne sont pas dangereuses et enragées. ... Chacun chez soi, sur sa terre et dans sa hutte, est maître de soi, debout et entier, sans que rien le courbe ou l'entame. ... *L'Anglais moderne est déjà tout entier dans ce Saxon.*[64] [emphasis added]

When Taine expounded these ideas they were not intended to be interpreted as anglophobic; today, however, they appear to form the basis of rather crude stereotypes. So influential were they, however, that they continued to be recycled in the *fin-de-siècle* by other widely read authors such as Alfred Fouillée, a self-professed admirer of Taine, who applied racially-derived arguments to his own notions of 'national psychology'. For example, in a key work published in 1903, Fouillée wrote of the English:

Aujourd'hui, la Grande Bretagne est partagée entre les éléments liguro-celtiques et les éléments germaniques, mais ceux-ci ont conservé un notable avantage. Le type brun à tête large reprend cependant le dessus dans les villes, depuis plusiers siècles, et finira par exercer son influence envahissante. Le mélange de sang celto-ligure et de sang germain, qui, pour l'anthropologie, rend la Grande Bretagne si analogue à la Gaule antique, est peut-être la raison pour laquelle le tempérament anglais, quoique souvent flegmatique [sic], est plus nerveux que celui du Germain pur.[65]

The continuing influence of Taine in respect of *climat* and *milieu*, although somewhat attenuated, is very clear in these pages:

Taine ... a insisté outre mesure sur les effets du climat. Ce qu'on peut lui accorder, c'est que le ciel humide et froid de l'Angleterre a renforcé les influences qui font de l'acquisition d'un certain bien-être individuel le but le plus nécessaire pour tous. On a calculé que la nourriture d'un seul Anglais suffirait à une famille de huit personnes en Grèce. ... La situation insulaire devait aussi exercer une grande action et sur les destinées et sur l'esprit du peuple anglais; elle tendait à l'isoler en soi. D'une part, elle l'obligeait à une fusion plus rapide et plus complète de ses éléments intérieurs, qui devait produire plus vite un caractère un et homogène; d'autre part, elle empêchait à l'extérieur des communications qui auraient eu pour résultat une sociabilité plus étendue.[66]

For Fouillée, who published these thoughts a year before the conclusion of the *Entente*, the English communicated with the Continent solely for the purposes of conquering territory, or for the conduct of commerce.[67] Again, the tone of this work is certainly not anglophobic in the way that Jacques Bonhomme's view is in the Larousse dictionary entry; but the assumptions, stereotypes and supposed national characteristics are all still present. The illusory, or evanescent, nature of English 'national character', or 'racial type', is well illustrated in a fundamental and complex paradox recognized by Fouillée.

Pour bien comprehende la direction et le développement propre du caractère anglais, il faut se rappeler que la race germanique, dont les Anglo-Saxons étaient une branche, a fini par présenter une double antithèse, qui est devenue sa marque distinctive: intérieurement, contraste du réalisme et d'un certain idéalisme mystique; dans ses rapports sociaux, conciliation de l'individualisme et du goût pour la subordination hiérarchique. Les Anglo-Saxons avaient sans doute les mêmes tendances que les autres Germains, mais leurs penchants furent modifiés, d'abord par l'influence celtique et normande, puis par les conditions de leur développement national.[68]

The *Entente Cordiale* marked something of a turning point, of course, not just in the field of Anglo-French diplomatic relations but also in this field of 'national psychology'. Works such as Fouillée's inspired other writers, Jean Finot for instance, to challenge such notions.[69] Finot preferred to talk of an 'Anglo-French nation', and criticized what he called the 'legend of the peoples called Latin'. In the preface to the English translation of his book on *Race Prejudice*, he referred to the racism and atavistic hatred based on spurious pseudo-science which had spoiled Anglo-French relations for so long, and which had created an atmosphere of virtually irreconcilable hostility, so much so that Finot's work was reportedly mocked by those who preferred the simplistic racial divisions.[70] On the English side of the Channel, Finot's attempts to discredit racial differences between Latin and Saxon found an influential propagator in W.T.Stead, editor of the *Review of Reviews*. In 1911 Stead prefaced a translation of Finot's *Death Agony of the 'Science' of Race*. He underlined the fact that until twelve years previously, 'the pseudo-scientific theory of the mental and radical differences of Races was almost universally accepted', and that Finot's work had proved to be as 'potent as the blast of horns in Jericho'. Stead applauded the new view that there was 'no such thing as race', that men were 'indivisible', and that Finot had 'revolutionized the scientific concept of the race question'.[71]

Later experience showed, however, that simplistic prejudices would prove to be extremely tenacious on both sides of the Channel. In 1920, the British Foreign Office was advising the Cabinet on whether to proceed with a Channel tunnel project. Hardly any time at all after the French and British had been fighting side by side against the Germans, and at a moment when they were 'still Allies in the field', in order to underline their case *against* the project (when even naval and military authorities had expressed no objections), the authors of a memorandum invoked the age-old hostility between the two nations. [In the quotations below the emphasis is added.]

The whole question is dependent upon the stability of friendly relations between France and this country. If we could be convinced that we and the French would maintain a perpetual friendship and never quarrel, then it is obvious that there would be a distinct advantage in having a tunnel, although the economic advantages to be obtained from it are not so real as might be imagined. Consequently the question resolves itself into that of relations in the near and distant future.

They came to the heart of the problem:

It must be remembered that until a century ago France was England's historic and natural enemy, and that *a real friendship between the inhabitants of the two countries had always been very difficult owing to differences of language, mentality and national character*. These differences are not likely to decrease. The slightest incident may arouse the resentment or jealousy of the French and fan the latent embers of suspicion into a flame. Nor can Great Britain place any reliance upon public opinion in France being well balanced and reasonable. It is within the memory of many of us that in 1893, when there was trouble with France over the boundaries of Siam, war was within an ace of being provoked by the aggressive entry of Admiral Humann with his gunboats into

the Menam River. ... It was only the coolness and self-restraint of the British officer in command that prevented a conflict.
Thus the historical context, 'within the memory of many' at the Foreign Office, completely predetermined their view:

> It is almost certain that we shall have conflicts with France in the future as we have in the past. ... *Nothing can alter the fundamental fact that we are not liked in France, and never will be, except for the advantages which the French people may be able to extract from us.* These considerations point conclusively to the imprudence, and even danger, of increasing at enormous cost the facilities of communication with France by means of a tunnel under the Channel which may have to be destroyed at any moment as a military measure to secure the safety of this country in the event of France assuming a hostile and aggressive attitude.

The price that would have to be paid for this improved 'communication' would be far too high. The memorandum's conclusion betrays a lingering fondness for 'splendid isolation' at the Foreign Office:

> The Foreign Office conclusion is that our relations with France never have been, are not, and probably never will be, sufficiently stable and friendly to justify the construction of a Channel tunnel, and the loss of security which our insular position, even in spite of the wonderful scientific and mechanical developments of recent years, still continues to bestow.[72]

This text is remarkable because it is not expressed in the emotional language of xenophobic nationalism: the case rests, interestingly enough, on what the authors of the memorandum – like the French writers quoted above – pinpoint as fundamental and irreconcilable *differences* between the two countries. In other words, because of their different 'national character', French and British *identities* are irreconcilable.

This area of the history of Anglo-French relations – the area beyond the diplomatic – and other related fields, such as debates on superiority-inferiority complexes and themes dominating public opinion in the two nations, all call for further research.[73] Indeed an objective history of the way the French and the British have perceived and portrayed each other, at different levels of society and culture, is long overdue.

Notes

I should like to thank Peter Morris for his comments on an early draft of this essay.

1. The proceedings have been published: see especially M. Cornick, *'Faut-il réduire l'Angleterre en esclavage?* A case study of French anglophobia, October 1935', in *Franco-British Studies* 14 (Autumn 1992) pp.3-19.
2. F. Crouzet, 'Problèmes de la communication franco-britannique aux XIXe et XXe siècles', *Revue historique* 254 (1975) pp.105-34.
3. Pierre Birnbaum has examined this exclusive, reductionist, nationalism in a Franco-French context in *'La France aux Français!' Les haines nationalistes en France* (Paris, 1993).
4. The expression was used by Georges Berry, député for Paris, in a speech entitled 'Français-Boers' given in March 1900. See Henri Cyral, *France et Transvaal. L'opinion française* (Paris, 1902) p.250.
5. F. Braudel, *Identité de la France* (2 vols to date, Paris, 1986-).
6. The British relationship with Europe remains one of the most contentious issues today; see J. Julliard, 'Chers ennemis héréditaires (Lettre aux Anglais sur l'Europe)', *Nouvel Observateur*, 1464 (26 November 1992). Uses of the myth spring up quite unexpectedly: see the reports in the French and British press on allegations that the French counter-espionage service, the DST, apprehended MI6 agents spying on the construction at Brest of the aircraft-carrier *Charles de Gaulle (Journal du dimanche*, 22 August 1993, and *The Guardian,* 23 August 1993).
7. Jean-Louis Crémieux-Brilhac, *Les Français de l'an 40* (2 vols, Paris, 1990) vol.1, *La guerre oui ou non?* pp.19-20.
8. Pierre Milza notes that 'son audience n'est ... nullement limitée aux milieux d'extrême-droite'; *Le fascisme italien et la presse française* (Brussels, 1987) p.266.
9. Eugen Weber provides an extensive catalogue of these in 'Of stereotypes and of the French', *Journal of Contemporary History* 25 (1990) pp.169-203. The role played by 'national characteristics' and stereotypes in international relations has been variously examined; see, for example, J.-B. Duroselle, 'Opinion, attitude, mentalité, mythe, idéologie: essai de clarification', *Relations Internationales* 2 (1974) pp.3-23; S. Friedländer, '"Mentalité collective" et "caractère national": une étude systématique est-elle possible?', in ibid., pp.25-35; P. Guillen, 'Opinion publique et politique extérieure en France, 1914-1940'

in *Opinion publique et politique extérieure 1915-1940* (Rome, 1982) pp.37-56.

10. P. Rickard, *Britain in Medieval French Literature* (Oxford, 1956) p.183. I am grateful to Professor Christopher Allmand of Liverpool University for indicating this reference.

11. Ibid., chapter 7 passim.

12. C. Beaune, *Naissance de la nation France* (Paris, 1985) pp.38, 40, 44, 355.

13. Ibid., p.44.

14. Rickard, *Britain in Medieval French Literature* p.44.

15. See also Michel Winock, 'Jeanne d'Arc', in P. Nora (ed.), *Les lieux de mémoire* (3 vols, Paris, 1984-1992), vol.3 *Les France*, pt.3 *De l'archive à l'emblème* pp.675-733.

16. 'The last decade or so of the nineteenth century continued to produce works which, while based solidly on archive material and on the chronicles printed by the 'Sociéte de l'Histoire de France' and other, local societies, were to maintain an underlying anti-English tone': C.T. Allmand, *Lancastrian Normandy, 1415-1450. The history of a medieval occupation* (Oxford,1983) p.308.

17. 'Having invented the nation, the French had to invent national definition and identification': Weber, 'Of Stereotypes' p.181.

18. Mona Ozouf, *La fête révolutionnaire, 1789-1799* (Paris, 1976).

19. See, for instance, J. Godechot, *Le comte d'Antraigues: un espion dans l'empire des émigrés* (Paris, 1986).

20. *Poésies révolutionnaires et contre-révolutionnaires, ou recueil, classé par époques, des hymnes, chants guerriers, chansons républicaines, odes, satires, cantiques, etc. Les plus remarquables qui ont parues depuis 30 ans* (2 vols, Paris, 1821).

21. Ibid., vol.1, pp.159-60. The reference to the calendar is made by Geneviève Tabouis in *Albion perfide ou loyale. De la guerre de cent ans à nos jours* (Paris, 1938) p.46. The lines were adapted thus: 'Attaquons dans ses eaux, la perfide Albion! Que nos fastes s'ouvrent par sa destruction et marquent les jours de la victoire!'

22. *Poésies révolutionnaires* vol.1, p.169.

23. Ibid., p.185.

24. The first of these, held on 14 July 1790, was attended by 60,000 delegates from all the 83 departments into which France had been divided.

25. '"La reprise de Toulon", hymne chanté à la fête du Champs de Mars, le 10 nivôse, an II', in *Poésies révolutionnaires* vol.1, pp.205-6.

26. Ibid., pp.246-7. The heroic but hopeless resistance of the *Vengeur* took place on 13 prairial, an II.

27. Ibid., p.266; 'Le Salpêtre'.

28. *Poésies révolutionnaires* vol.2, pp.31-4.

29. '"La couronne de Napoléon", chant impérial, distribué par ordre de la Préfecture de Police, le 2 décembre 1804, jour du couronnement', in ibid., p.65.

30. 'This expansion of patriotism ... meant ushering the masses into national politics; or, rather, bringing politics into the life of the masses. ... Stereotypes, culled from history, would reinforce the tendency to relate national unity to national character, national character to natural forces that determine that character and the policies of the nation ...': Weber, 'Of stereotypes' pp.181-2.

31. Pierre Larousse, *Grand Dictionnaire Universel*, tome premier [1864], 'Préface'. Larousse's encyclopaedic dictionary has begun to attract critical attention and has been republished in its entirety: see Jean-Yves Mollier, 'Pierre Larousse, sa vie, son dictionnaire', in *L'Histoire* 165 (1993) pp.66-8.

32. Larousse, *Grand Dictionnaire Universel*, Tome premier [1864], 'A', pp. 176, 361-2, 363-77.

33. Ibid., p.176 [col.3].

34. Ibid., p.361 [col.3].

35. Ibid., [col.4].

36. Ibid., p.374 [col.4].

37. Ibid., p.375 [col.1].

38. Ibid., p.375 [col.2].

39. Ibid., p.376 [col.1].

40. Ibid., [col.2]. Cf. the anecdote referred to above (note 35).

41. Ibid.

42. Ibid., [col.4].

43. On Verne's fiction, see Jean Chesneaux, *Lecture politique des romans de Jules Verne* (Paris, 1971).

44. A. Assolant, *Aventures merveilleuses, mais authentiques, du Capitaine Corcoran* (2 vols, Paris, 1867). Assolant was a prolific author of such pulp fiction.

45. Cf. Rickard, *Britain in Medieval French Literature*, passim, esp. chapter 8. Indeed, Pierre Larousse cites in his bibliography a widely used anglophobic text by a Breton author, A. Kervigan, *L'Angleterre telle qu'elle est* (Paris, 1860). For a modern view of the same tradition, see the autobiographical text by Alain Robbe-Grillet, *Le miroir qui revient* (Paris, 1984) pp.113 ff.

46. Assolant, *Aventures merveilleuses*, vol.1, pp.70-1.

47. Ibid., vol.2, p.316.

48. It is worth noting in passing that the prehistory of this bizarre tale of intrigue in the Indian subcontinent is traced in the second part to an episode dating from

Napoleon's invasion of Egypt, when he was supposedly meditating the conquest of India. There is a reference to a certain Lascaris, an actual historical character mentioned by Lamartine in his *Voyage en Orient*, who, according to the narrator, would have resembled Talleyrand had Napoleon succeeded in conquering the English and the Russians (Assolant, vol.2, p.141).

49. Paul d'Ivoi, *Le Sergent Simplet à travers les colonies françaises* (Paris, 1895). The work appeared in several subsequent reprints well into the 1900s. Paul d'Ivoi was a pseudonym for Paul Deleutre.

50. Ibid., p.242.

51. Ibid.

52. Ibid.

53. Ibid., p.288. For the effect of this clash on the Foreign Office, see below, pp.27-8.

54. See the following: E. Demolins, *A quoi tient la supériorité des Anglo-Saxons?* (Paris, 1897); C. Crespin, *Les Français sont-ils inférieurs aux Anglais? A propos d'un livre de M. E. Demolins* (Verneuil, 1898); Anold [pseudonym], *A quoi tient la supériorité des Français sur les Anglo-Saxons?* (Paris, 1899); L. Bazalgette, *A quoi tient l'infériorité française?* (Paris, 1900).

55. Capitaine Danrit, *Guerre maritime et sous-marine* (Paris, 1908). Danrit was an anagrammatic pseudonym of Commandant Emile-Augustin-Cyprien Driant who, if one reads his entry in the BN catalogue, was clearly obsessed and tantalized by the idea of a future war with England.

56. Capitaine Danrit, *Guerre fatale, France-Angleterre* (2 vols, Paris, 1902; reprinted 1903).

57. Danrit, *Guerre maritime et sous-marine* p.52.

58. The French pro-Boer movement and the anglophobia which it inspired await their historian; for some examples, see H. Cyral, *France et Transvaal. L'opinion française* (Paris, 1902). On the exploits of Villebois de Mareuil, see R. McNab, *The French Colonel* (Oxford, 1975).

59. For details of the racial 'origin myths' of France and England, see L. Poliakov, *The Aryan Myth. A History of Racist and Nationalist Ideas in Europe* (London, 1974), chapters 2-3. Eugen Weber examines the prevalence of these determining ideas in French historiography in 'Nos ancêtres les Gaulois', *My France* (Cambridge, Mass., 1991) pp.21-39.

60. E.g., in J.A. Gobineau, *Essai sur l'inégalité des races humaines* (Paris, 1853).

61. On Thierry, see Weber, 'Nos ancêtres', and H. Taine, *Histoire de la littérature anglaise* (Paris, 1864), and also his *Notes sur l'Angleterre* (Paris, 1872).

62. Taine, *Histoire* (12th edition, 5 vols, Paris, 1905-1906) vol.1, p.xliii.

63. See V. Giraud, *Essai sur Taine, son oeuvre et son influence* (Paris, 1901); F.-C. Roe, *Taine et l'Angleterre* (Paris, 1923).

64. Taine, *Histoire,* pp.6, 9, 15, 16.

65. A. Fouillée, *Esquisse psychologique des peuples européens* (Paris, 1903) pp.192-3.

66. Ibid., pp.193-4.

67. Ibid., p.194.

68. Ibid., p.195.

69. Jean Finot's works include: *Français et Anglais. L'Angleterre malade – médecins et remèdes* (Paris, 1902); *Français et Anglais devant l'anarchie européenne* (Paris, 1904); *Le préjugé des races* (Paris, 1905), translated as *Race Prejudice* (London, 1906); *Civilisés contre Allemands. La grande croisade,* (Paris, 1915), of which chapter 10 was translated as *The Anglo-French Nation: a study in interpenetration* (London, 1916).

70. See the report of Finot's essays in *The Times* (1 Nov. 1902), and the preface to *Race Prejudice.*

71. W. Stead, preface to J. Finot, *Death Agony of the 'Science' of Race,* trans. C. Grande (London, 1911) pp.4, 6, 7.

72. Foreign Office Memorandum on the Channel tunnel, dated 1 May 1920, reproduced in E.L. Woodward, R. Butler et al. (eds), *Documents on British Foreign Policy, 1919-1939, First Series,* (27 vols, London, 1947-1986) vol.12, pp.39-40.

73. For instance, see Cornick, 'L'impact de l'affaire Dreyfus en Grande-Bretagne' in M. Drouin (ed.), *L'Affaire Dreyfus de A à Z* (Paris, 1994 forthcoming).

'Allies are a tiresome lot'
Britain, France and the Balkan Campaign 1915-18

David Dutton

Winston Churchill's judgement on the value of wartime alliances has become something of a commonplace. 'There is only one thing worse than fighting with allies', he asserted, 'and that is fighting without them.'[1] It seems probable that the experience of Britain's partnership with France in two world wars figured prominently in Churchill's assessment. Nor was this guarded enthusiasm for wartime partners simply the isolated sentiment of one, admittedly distinguished, individual. When George VI wrote to his mother after the fall of France in 1940, 'Personally I feel happier now that we have no allies to be polite to and to pamper', it seems certain that, however illogical in terms of any calculation of military advantage, the King was articulating a commonly-held sense of relief among his subjects.[2] Seven months later Britain was still without major allies. His Majesty's command of English syntax had deteriorated, but his feelings towards his erstwhile ally had not changed:

> I always feel that we have to be thankful France collapsed at once after Dunkirk, so that we were able to reorganize the Army at home, and gave us time to prepare the Air Force to repel the Blitzkrieg.[3]

George VI's father and predecessor had never had the opportunity to express comparable sentiments in the course of World War One. It was, of course, a feature – some would say a striking achievement – of the Anglo-French alliance in this first great conflict that it survived unbroken for the duration of hostilities. This should not, however, lead us to suppose that the absence of military catastrophe on a par with that of 1940 inevitably bred fond feelings for Britain's French partners. Sir William Robertson, Chief of the Imperial General Staff and a regular attender at wartime inter-allied conferences, was reputed to voice deep suspicion of and thinly veiled hostility towards colleagues who did not speak English. Significantly, his xenophobia was selective. 'If only we and the Boche were allies', Robertson is said to have remarked at one inter-allied gathering, 'how easily we could beat all this crowd!'[4] This story may quite possibly be apocryphal, but a study of

Robertson's wartime career only serves to enhance its credibility. In one private letter the CIGS – renowned more for the directness than the eloquence of his prose – certainly did assert that 'allies are a tiresome lot'.[5]

The aspect of the war which, above all others, probably prompted Robertson's observation was the Anglo-French military expedition to the Balkans. Robertson's sober assessment written in his retirement was that 'of all the problems which brought soldiers and statesmen into conference during the years 1915-17, the Salonica expedition was at once the most persistent, exasperating and unfruitful'.[6] Launched with the despatch of British and French troops to the Greek port of Salonica in October 1915, the campaign remained in being for the rest of the war. In much of the historiography of the First World War it merits only cursory treatment, a forgotten army, but contemporaries could scarcely ignore the existence of a force which at times approached half a million men. For most of its lifetime, however, the expedition seemed to lack military purpose and its continuation was a source of mystery and confusion to those who looked on. That it was from France, a country which fought the entire war with enemy troops firmly entrenched on its soil, that most enthusiasm for the campaign derived, only compounded the sense of puzzlement. Writing in 1918, the war correspondent G. Ward Price commented:

> My own opinion is that until all the documents now held secret in different countries ... are revealed there will be very few men indeed who know the inside story of the Allies' doings in the Balkans, these two years past.[7]

Though the Anglo-French Entente had existed since 1904, British politicians had carefully resisted the entreaties of their French opposite numbers for a binding military engagement between the two countries and the alliance was purely the product of the coming of war. In such circumstances it is perhaps not surprising that two countries which took pride in their own independence were slow to work out the practicalities of a wartime coalition. Though the desire to defeat the German enemy imposed a certain unity of purpose, this could not disguise differing ideas about the means of securing this objective nor the wish to fulfil conflicting ambitions, many of which predated the comparatively recent rapprochement between the two countries. In the absence of an established institution to co-ordinate a political and military strategy, the leaders of Britain and France could do little more than substitute a seemingly endless series of inter-allied conferences. Yet, as experience showed, this was a most imperfect arrangement. As Arthur Balfour noted:

> What impresses me most painfully is the futility ... of our various international conferences. They have not been few in number, but in many cases the resolutions – long discussed and embodied in formal minutes duly signed by the governments concerned – have been departed from as soon as the Conference separated.[8]

In like vein the influential Lord Esher commented on the sorry state of Anglo-French co-ordination in the light of the launching of the Balkan campaign in the autumn of 1915. He called for a small and efficient directing staff of the ablest British and French officers, naval, military and political, who could so marshal and evaluate facts and ideas that the inferences drawn from them would be indisputable and certain to control the executive actions of the two nations. Existing arrangements had only led to 'hurried conferences, obscured counsels, vague and conflicting purposes, followed by decisions and counter-decisions'.[9]

* * *

Though the expedition to the Balkans was launched with almost indecent haste in the autumn of 1915, the actual idea of extending military operations to this part of Europe had a more respectable pedigree. As is well known, by the end of 1914 a distinguished triumvirate in the British war directorate – Winston Churchill, David Lloyd George and Colonel Maurice Hankey – were, independently of one another, starting to challenge the futility of offensive operations on the Western Front. Two of them – Lloyd George and Hankey – voiced an interest in the Balkans as an alternative theatre of war. At very much the same time the French cabinet minister, Aristide Briand, was producing a plan to send an allied force of perhaps 400,000 men to Salonica so as to protect Serbia, influence the other Balkan states and bring about an attack on the southern flank of the Austro-Hungarian Empire.[10] Within the French military elite similar ideas were being voiced by General

Franchet d'Espérey.[11]

Now it is true that most of these plans had not been fully thought through. Lloyd George was in this respect typical. Arguing that there was no prospect of breaching 'the carefully prepared German lines in the west', he wanted to extend the enemy's front and win 'a definite victory somewhere' in order to rally domestic opinion in Britain and attract wavering neutrals.[12] All this was commendable as far as it went, but, as Trevor Wilson has pointed out, Lloyd George's notion that Germany might be defeated by 'knocking the props under her' involved allowing an optimistic 'piece of kite-flying' to get in the way of the rational discussion of military practicalities. To talk of props whose removal would entail Germany's collapse 'constituted little more than a slight of hand with a wall map – upon which [Austria-Hungary and Turkey] appear "below" Germany'.[13]

But at least at this stage of the war the idea of a Balkan campaign was being discussed in terms of its possible military advantage to the Allies in their struggle against Germany. That the project was not taken much further is easily explained. After showing an apparent willingness to join the allied cause, the Greek Prime Minister, Eleutherios Venizelos, made it clear that Greece would not participate unless Roumania did so too. With Bulgaria drawing closer to Germany, the possibility of a Balkan coalition began to disappear. By the beginning of March 1915 few in either Britain or France still regarded a campaign in the Balkans as a practical proposition. The Allies were in any case now fully committed to operations at the Dardanelles – and one military (or in this case largely naval) sideshow was probably enough. As 1915 progressed, the failure of this venture served progressively to dampen the enthusiasm of many of those who had believed that a cheap victory in the war was there for the taking if only the right decisions were made.

None the less, it could be argued that, early in 1915, the idea of a campaign based on Salonica, designed to unite the forces of the Balkan states against the Central Powers, was at least an initiative which demanded careful consideration. By the time that the expedition finally materialised in October, however, it was as a last minute expedient dictated above all else by considerations of French internal politics and undertaken with almost no technical evaluation of its strategic possibilities. The key factor was the emergence in the summer of 1915 of a potential rival to the French commander-in-chief, General Joffre. The details of *l'affaire Sarrail* have been well documented elsewhere and need not be repeated here.[14] It seems certain that renewed French enthusiasm for an Eastern theatre of war was primarily a function of the determination to get Sarrail out of France. As one French observer confessed, 'il faut éloigner le général Sarrail même au prix d'une armée'.[15]

What, however, is particularly striking in the present context is the manner in which Britain agreed to follow France into this venture and later to maintain her commitment in the face of prevailing military wisdom. Between July and September of 1915 French politicians and generals debated the possibility of sending Sarrail to the East at the head of a substantial force. His command, however, was to be a reinvigorated campaign at the Dardenelles and not a new one at Salonica. While Joffre was keen to see Sarrail leave France, he was not willing to give him the level of reinforcements for which Sarrail asked, since this might weaken his own position on the main front. Moreover, Joffre's status within the French war directorate, though weaker than a year earlier, was still formidable. His opinions could not be lightly overruled. Sarrail, on the other hand, still perhaps hankering after a command in France which would leave open the possibility of his own eventual accession to Joffre's place, was unwilling to leave France except in circumstances which made it abundantly clear that he was not being exiled. This impasse proved difficult to resolve, but the repeated postponement of operations at the Straits into the winter months made their ultimate materialisation increasingly improbable. Prime Minister René Viviani reached the conclusion that 'l'opération des Dardanelles ne se fera pas. Le GQG ne veut pas qu'elle se fasse, parce que c'est le général Sarrail qui commande.'[16]

It was in this still fluid situation that the rapid development of diplomatic events in the Balkans intervened to overtake the internal wranglings in France. The mobilisation of the Bulgarian army rendered irrelevant any further discussion of renewing operations at the Dardanelles and recreated the prospect of a Balkan campaign, such as had been discussed at the beginning of the year. But the speed with which the French government now gave up its existing plans and seized upon the idea of an expedition to Salonica is a clear indication that the dominant consideration was not so much military strategy as the desire to be rid of Sarrail.

Sofia decreed general mobilisation on 23 September. Bulgaria, longing for revenge against Serbia since the Second Balkan War of 1913, was prepared to throw in its lot with the Central Powers in the belief that Austria too was ready to move south. The Serbian government, under the very real threat of being overrun, appealed immediately to London and Paris for aid, while from Greece Venizelos called for allied assistance to enable his country to honour its treaty obligations to Serbia. The French minister in Athens, Guillemin, had already discussed the possibility of an allied expedition based on Salonica with Venizelos. He understood that the Greek king would feel obliged to make a formal protest against the violation of his country's neutrality, but that the Greek government would in fact 'allow its hand to be forced'.[17] So when the news of Bulgarian mobilisation came through, Guillemin forwarded Venizelos' urgent request to the Quai d'Orsay that the Allies should provide 150,000 men, adding that Venizelos hoped that a reply would be made within twenty-four hours and significantly that the replies from London and Paris would be made without consultation between the two governments.[18] Guillemin urged acceptance of Venizelos' proposal, arguing that if the Allies did not respond the armed assistance of Greece would be lost for the duration of the war.[19]

Despite some resistance on the part of Foreign Minister Théophile Delcassé, the French cabinet agreed on 22 September to inform Venizelos that France was ready for her part to supply the troops which the Greek leader had requested.[20] The decision had been taken in some haste – and it was one which belonged to the politicians. Joffre merely acquiesced with the result that the campaign got underway with a total lack of strategic planning and forethought. Just as importantly, no attempt had been made to co-ordinate a response with Britain. Indeed, Paul Cambon, the French ambassador in London, argued that the French decision was somewhat premature in view of the fact that no prior agreement had been reached with Lord Kitchener, the British War Minister.[21] France's decision had been arrived at, as Venizelos had urged, without reference to London. Only when the French commitment had been made, was Cambon instructed to express the hope that the British government would make a similar offer to

Venizelos.[22]

Venizelos' appeal found British opinion divided. Hankey, for one, was clear that 'the idea of committing the Allies to yet another campaign in this part of the world ... is most objectionable from a military point of view'.[23] But the Foreign Secretary, Edward Grey, argued that, while it was not possible for Britain to send a force to Greece immediately, this might not be ruled out later on.[24] Some ministers felt inhibited from taking a decision as a result of Kitchener's temporary absence from London. Lloyd George, on the other hand, felt no such constraints. Reviving his old enthusiasm for a Balkan campaign, he produced wildly optimistic calculations to suggest that an intervention by 150,000 allied troops would result in the adhesion of 500-600,000 Roumanians and possibly 200,000 troops from Serbia and 150,000 from Greece. These figures totalled up to not far short of one million men, whom the Austro-Germans would have to attack, which in winter would be a very difficult operation. Surely, Lloyd George argued, it was worth sending 150,000 men to reap so rich a reward.[25]

By 24 September, however, the British government had effectively been presented with a *fait accompli* by their French allies. Ministers and officials went through the motions of evaluating the advantages and disadvantages of the proposed new venture, but in practice their options were now extremely limited. The Dardanelles Committee unanimously agreed that the British government should associate itself with the reply of France guaranteeing the forces requested to enable Greece to fulfil its pledge to Serbia. Prime Minister Asquith summed up what had happened in a subsequent letter to the King: 'The French at once agreed to comply and ... it was impossible for us in the circumstances to hold back.'[26] In the course of the meeting, however, Kitchener read out an appreciation drawn up by the General Staff. Its wording merits attention since it defined the limits within which British military authorities were prepared to accept a second eastern front – limits which, if adhered to, would have soon put a stop to the essentially futile confinement of large numbers of British troops in this unproductive theatre for the remainder of the war. The document read:

> It must be clearly understood that the role of the 150,000
> allied troops for which Greece has asked and which will,
> if necessary, be sent to Salonica will ... be restricted to

enabling and assisting the Greek army to protect the
Serbian flank and the line of communication with
Salonica.[27]

It was not long before the relevance of the British reservations became
apparent. Just before the first allied troops actually landed at Salonica,
Venizelos resigned, finding his position in relation to the Greek monarch,
King Constantine, untenable. So the Anglo-French force which was arriving
in Greece in order to enable that country to fulfil its obligations to Serbia,
was likely to confront a Greek army, in the process of mobilisation, which
would at best be neutral and which might – granted Constantine's personal
and family sympathies for the German cause – even prove hostile.

In this way the whole supposed justification for British intervention in the
Balkans – to assist the Greeks to fulfil a specific treaty obligation – had been
undermined, and the logic of the situation was that Britain should now either
withdraw completely or conform to the rather more extensive plans of
operations apparently envisaged by France. A statement of these French plans
was sent by Joffre to Kitchener on 9 October. Here it was argued that the
mission of the troops should be to cover and hold the railway line between
Salonica and Uskub in order to secure communication with the Serbian army
and the supplies of that army, while preventing any enemy attack on central
Serbia.[28] The divergence which was beginning to emerge between the
conceptions of the two governments was further revealed when Viviani
attempted to gain British approval for a statement of explanation which he
intended to make to the Chamber of Deputies on 12 October. The British did
not like any mention of 'assistance to Serbia' without reference to the original
Greek invitation, since they believed that without Greek cooperation Serbia
could only be saved by a really large allied force, which would be most
unlikely to arrive in time. The declaration, as Viviani proposed to make it,
seemed more like an open-ended commitment by Britain and France rather
than the clearly defined involvement which the British government was
prepared to accept.[29]

The British cabinet was, in fact, deeply divided. One group, which
included Lloyd George, was keen to continue sending troops to Salonica,
while another, including Kitchener, wanted to follow the advice of the
General Staff and make a renewed effort at the Dardanelles.[30] With the aim

of forcing the British government to come to a clear decision, the French War Minister, Alexandre Millerand, arrived in London on 15 October. He and his colleagues were concerned that, according to reports received from General Sarrail, the British troops were showing every intention of remaining at Salonica during the winter months instead of pressing north in support of the Serbs.[31] The military situation was deteriorating daily as the plight of Serbia became even more desperate. As the Serbian legation in London confirmed, the Serbian army on its own was not strong enough to withstand the enormous pressure exerted by the combined forces of Germany, Austria and Bulgaria.[32] Millerand now bluntly asserted that if the British did not continue to send troops to Salonica the French government would fall and the alliance itself would be endangered.

British military leaders looked on askance. Major-General Charles Callwell, the Director of Military Operations, felt that the French must be in abject terror of Sarrail and of their public opinion, which fondly imagined that saving the Serbs was a perfectly simple operation. In fact, according to Callwell, the task of the expedition was an impossible one. The French plans did not appear to have been properly thought out by the General Staff and he could not understand how they proposed to manage for transport.[33] Callwell assured General Robertson, who was anxiously watching the situation from headquarters in France, that the British General Staff were totally opposed to operations in the Balkans which were 'objectionable from every point of view'.[34] Robertson took heart from this statement and urged that Britain should beware of having her hand forced by Millerand or any other French politician. He considered that strained relations with the French would be preferable to losing two or three divisions in the Balkans and perhaps even losing the war.[35]

But Millerand's dire warnings of possible political chaos in France were confirmed by reports from the British embassy in Paris. There Lord Bertie noted that French public opinion might well become exasperated if the British showed any signs of backing out of the Salonica expedition. Joffre had expressed the view that it was necessary, both from military and political points of view, to continue operations based on Salonica and indeed to send additional troops.[36] Inside the British Foreign Office the Permanent Under-Secretary, Sir Arthur Nicolson, concluded that 'our relations with France will be seriously impaired if we do not meet their wishes by sending immediately the division to Salonica'.[37]

The effect which all this pressure was having on the British government became apparent when the Dardanelles Committee met on 25 October to consider the Balkan situation. This meeting was crucial in exposing the reality of the British position. The nature of the decisions reached, and more particularly that of the arguments used to support them, go far to explain that British readiness to acquiesce in French policy decisions which would characterise the country's conduct of the campaign as a whole. At the meeting Kitchener announced that he had received a strongly worded note from the French Military Attaché requesting that British troops should be sent immediately to Salonica, since any delay would mean the destruction of the Serbian army. In Kitchener's opinion the terms in which the French note was couched suggested that there was a political motive behind it and that it was not entirely based on the requirements of strategy. The question which arose in his mind, therefore, was whether a refusal on Britain's part to comply with French demands would place the French government in any political difficulty. Grey wondered whether Joffre really thought the expedition strategically sound, or whether he was obliged to back it for other reasons, possibly the fear that otherwise Millerand would fall and the barrier protecting Joffre from criticism in the French chamber be removed.[38] To this Kitchener added that if Millerand resigned, Joffre would not be able to maintain his own position, a development which would entail considerable changes in the policy of France. His advice, therefore, was that the British government should tell the French that they intended to take the correct course, but that if this involved any danger of upsetting the French government, they would send the troops asked for to Salonica.

Sir John French, hastily summoned from his headquarters in France, then expounded upon the internal French political situation in a way which revealed that the British were fully acquainted with the intricacies of 'l'affaire Sarrail'.[39] The picture drawn was of a very delicate structure, which any false move by France's ally might serve to upset. This description provoked a pertinent question from Austen Chamberlain, Secretary of State for India. If the Salonica expedition was a futile military operation, he asked, was it worthwhile going on with it in order to save Millerand, Joffre and the French government. But political and military issues could not be separated that easily. Kitchener, whose priorities were necessarily military, answered with ponderous authority that more was at stake than Chamberlain seemed to appreciate – it was to save the alliance itself. If France were to break with Britain, the war would be over and Britain defeated.[40]

The implications of this meeting were considerable for, though it would not have been appreciated at the time, Britain was effectively abdicating its right to have any more than a nominal voice in the direction of allied strategy in the Balkans. The principle had been established that the maintenance of the existing régime in France should have priority over all other military and diplomatic considerations in this theatre of war. It meant that France could justify all future development of and modifications to her policy in this area, and secure the adherence of the British to them, on arguments relating to the stability of her own domestic political situation. In adopting this principle, Britain was in danger of enveloping her freedom of manoeuvre in the Balkans in a paralysing cocoon of submission to the will of her ally – and this is precisely what happened at least until the spring of 1917. All attempts to reassert a degree of independence and sovereign authority in British policy towards the Salonica enterprise were doomed to be quashed for fear of their disrupting effect on the other side of the Channel.

British military opinion never wavered from the conviction that the Salonica expedition represented a waste of valuable resources. In November 1915, shortly before he was superseded as CIGS, General A.J. Murray put forward the views of the General Staff on the existing situation in the Balkans. Murray did not mince his words. 'As to holding Salonica', he said,

> the General Staff have no hesitation whatever in urging that it should be vacated, and as quickly as possible ... The only argument for holding it that is worth considering is to deprive the enemy of a submarine base. We cannot for a moment consider that as a sufficient justification for locking up an army of 150,000 men ... The weight of military arguments against holding Salonica is overwhelming ....[41]

Early the following month the British actually believed that they had persuaded their French colleagues in conference at Calais to abandon the campaign. Within days, however, they were forced to change course when

Paris made it known that a political crisis in the French government would result if the British did not give way.[42]

Hankey could scarcely contain the contempt he felt for his political masters:

> The Government are really dreadfully to blame. They put off decisions, squabble, have no plans of action or operation, and allowed themselves to be dragged into this miserable Salonica affair at the tail of French domestic politics. I see only one solution – to suspend the constitution and appoint a dictator.[43]

That dictatorship never, of course, materialised, though some historians have argued that Murray's successor as CIGS, Sir William Robertson, came near to achieving such a state of affairs at the head of British war strategy in the course of 1916.[44] It is certainly true that Robertson, who replaced Murray in December 1915, was given unprecedented powers in his new post – largely at the behest of politicians who sought to counter-balance Kitchener's overweening influence within the making of British policy. But any notion of a 'Robertson dictatorship', however valid in relation to the Western Front, needs to take account of his relative inability to get his way over the Balkans.[45]

Robertson was capable of expressing his ideas with commendable simplicity. Shortly before becoming CIGS he wrote:

> The war may end either in the defeat of the Central Powers, in the defeat of the Entente, or in mutual exhaustion. The object of the Entente Powers is to bring about the first of these results, which can only be attained by the defeat or exhaustion of the predominant partner in the Central Alliance – Germany. Every plan of operation must therefore be examined from the point of view of its bearing on this result. If it is not, it will have a false basis, and will accordingly lead to false conclusions.[46]

The implications of these words for the future of the Salonica expedition are too obvious to be spelt out. But Robertson was never able to translate his wishes into action. With mounting irritation he condemned the failure of his political colleagues to assert themselves in relation to their French opposite numbers:

> The fact is that we are not taking nearly sufficient lead in
> the conduct of the war, considering the great amount we
> are contributing towards it ... We must take charge of the
> thing in politics in the same way as we are gradually
> beginning to do in military affairs ... They [the French]
> really are rather difficult people to deal with.[47]

But it was all to no avail. Salonica would go on, especially while Lloyd
George held high office, for he was slower than almost any other British
politician to lose his enthusiasm for a campaign in the Balkans. The British
contingent became the forgotten army of the Great War, effectively locked
up in what the Germans called 'the biggest internment camp in Europe'. Not
surprisingly, the overall contribution of the allied forces to their countries'
war effort was negligible. The real war, suggests one critic, 'was waged
against the malarial mosquito'.[48] Hopes rose in the autumn of 1916 when
Roumania finally aligned itself with the Allies. Such optimism, however, was
short-lived. In December, in the wake of Roumania's collapse, even an
enthusiast for the campaign was forced to concede that:

> The mishandling of the Balkan situation by the Allies is the
> most tragic and inexcusable feature of the history of the
> war ... As the inevitable result of these divided counsels,
> the Balkan situation has been allowed to drift from bad to
> worse, and there is a great deal that both the British and
> French Governments will have to answer for when the
> whole story is dragged into the light of day.[49]

* * *

To know that Britain's participation in the Salonica expedition was largely a
function of the requirements of French politics was certainly galling for the
majority of Britain's political and military leaders. But even if, as Robertson
argued, 'the whole thing is a French political rant', this situation was still
capable of rational analysis and justification.[50] If it was indeed true that any
attempt to withdraw troops from Salonica or to replace General Sarrail might
precipitate a governmental crisis in France, this was not a matter to be taken

lightly. The ending of France's wartime political truce – the so-called Sacred Union – might lead to an entirely different type of government emerging. British observers were understandably alarmed at the prospect of a cabinet headed by the Radical Socialist leader, Joseph Caillaux, for such a government might be willing to consider the possibilities of a negotiated peace with Germany. And such a development would make it virtually impossible for Britain to continue the fight alone. So, as Kitchener had pointed out to the Dardanelles Committee in October 1915, Britain was not really faced by a simple choice between what was politically expedient for France and what was militarily desirable for Britain.[51]

As the campaign progressed, however, a further and even less comfortable realisation dawned on British observers – that France might be using her presence in the Balkans to further long-term aims for the postwar world. British perceptions of what their French ally might be up to were vague and ill-defined. Gradually, however, the belief mounted that in some way or other the French were not really playing the game. Lord Kitchener, whom it was once usual to deride for his lack of understanding, was perhaps the first British leader to voice his misgivings. In March 1916 he warned his colleagues on the War Committee that the French were using the war for purposes of future expansion in the East.[52] The following week he suggested to Douglas Haig that France was aiming to develop her influence in the Eastern Mediterranean and would not now fight actively to beat the Germans in France.[53] Six months later, the new permanent head of the Foreign Office, Lord Hardinge, wrote in similar vein. He did not 'quite know what the French were up to in Greece'. But it appeared that they had some 'ulterior object in view' which was perhaps the aspiration to 'a sort of position of eventual protector of Greece in the Eastern Mediterranean'.[54]

Reviewing the problem for the Cabinet Committee on War Policy in the summer of 1917, Lord Milner preferred to shift the element of uncertainty on to the French themselves. He conceded that they were 'playing a game of their own', but did not believe that they quite knew what they wanted, except to exercise a predominant influence in Greece and to get some economic advantage out of it in the future. The policy was one of 'indefinite grab' and Sarrail was the living embodiment of it, being only interested in 'schemes of future exploitation'.[55] This emphasis on a financial motive was confirmed by observers on the spot, who were also able to give greater precision to their accusations. From Salonica itself General Milne also focussed attention on Sarrail and suggested that he was doing all he could for French interests in the Near-East after the war.[56] The French general paid little attention to the military front but was giving a good deal to Greece. The French wanted to occupy Thessaly, a base more commercial than military in its potential uses, to secure an outlet for French trade. This concern with the postwar world was evidently galling to the British commander, who argued that it was costing Britain a good deal in men, money and material, with no compensatory advantages, to get Greek affairs entirely into French hands with a view to French supremacy in the Eastern Mediterranean. Milne wondered how long the process of being made a catspaw was going to continue.[57] Even George V voiced concern about what was going on and was informed by Balfour that 'the Italians suspect the French and the French suspect the Italians of entertaining schemes (vague perhaps but not negligible) which will enable them respectively to use Greece as a pawn in the game of rivalry which they are playing in the Eastern Mediterranean'.[58]

But by far the clearest statement of the long-term aims of French policy in the Balkans was drawn up by the author Compton Mackenzie, then head of British intelligence in Greece, in the spring of 1917.[59] According to Mackenzie, 'Salonica was the expression of [French] aspirations in the Near East'[60] and, far from being a maverick general out of political control, Sarrail was but the agent of his government's schemes.[61] The French now wished to occupy Greece itself as a means of interfering with Italian aspirations in the Near-East. It was, Mackenzie concluded, time to stop Britain being used as the rubbing-rag of the ill-considered aspirations and unreasonable ambitions of two rival Latin nations.

The British ambassador in Greece, Sir Francis Elliot, was greatly impressed by Mackenzie's analysis and wrote enthusiastically to the Foreign Office in its support.[62] The previous November Elliot had warned Grey of the way in which France was determined to obtain complete control over Greece so as to use that country as a stepping stone between Marseilles and Syria.[63] Now, with the Foreign Office in new hands, Elliot reiterated that the French had a definite policy to bring Greece under their exclusive or at least predominant influence.[64] 'Both the French and the Italians', he argued, 'are constantly looking to the future and to the partition which is to come after the war, while we are devoting our whole faculties to the one object of winning it.'[65]

Inside the Foreign Office Mackenzie's report seemed initially to have a less conspicuous impact. George Clerk minuted that it was 'worth reading', but commented that Mackenzie lacked knowledge of the general political position of the British government. But Mackenzie's memorandum was clearly in the minds of Foreign Office officials as they reacted later that month to a despatch from Bertie in Paris, which indicated that the recent fall of the Briand government was likely to precipitate a stiffening of French policy in Greece. Harold Nicolson now argued that an early occasion should be taken to discuss with the French the essential objects of allied policy in Greece and to discover what they were really aiming at in the Near East. Discussions had previously been limited to the local problems of the moment, but Nicolson thought it clear that the French saw the issue in broader terms and that Greece was to play an important role in their future Mediterranean policy – a policy to which, on imperial grounds, Britain could not remain indifferent. The essential question, he concluded, was whether or not Britain was going to allow France to assume a protectorate over Greece and the Eastern Mediterranean. Despite his earlier reservations, George Clerk also showed the impact of Mackenzie's analysis. He argued that the time had come not only for a frank discussion with the French government about Greece, but also for Britain, when met as she would be by old arguments, to insist that the question of Greece was vital for Britain and that she would no longer tolerate the lines of present French action.[66]

With Foreign Secretary Balfour absent in America, Harold Nicolson drafted a long and detailed despatch to Bertie in Paris. After amendments by Hardinge and Balfour's deputy, Lord Robert Cecil, it was signed by the latter. The despatch argued that there was an urgent need for a full and frank discussion of the attitude to be adopted towards Greece. Though there was no specific indictment of French as opposed to British policy, the whole tone of the telegram was critical of French actions and suspicious of French motives. It was argued that the behaviour and language of several French agents in Greece had created the suspicion that an influential section of French opinion was keen to use the Balkan venture to secure something like a permanent protectorate over Greece.[67]

Had this telegram been despatched, it is just possible that Britain and France would finally have sorted out their longstanding, but often scarcely spoken, difficulties over the Salonica campaign. Bertie, however, had no opportunity to put the Foreign Office's observations before the French government. Lloyd George, now Prime Minister, was still unwilling to risk a political crisis in the alliance. On his intervention the despatch was never sent. The expedition in the Balkans continued for the duration. The most that the British government was able to achieve during 1917 was to reduce its own military contribution. Not until November 1917, when Georges Clemenceau, an avowed opponent of both the campaign and its commander, became French Prime Minister, was there a significant change. Sarrail was unceremoniously recalled on 10 December – with none of the dire political consequences for so long predicted. Yet still the campaign continued. Finally, on 15 September 1918, the Anglo-French army broke out of its confinement and swept north towards the Danube. Bulgaria quickly collapsed and signed an armistice on 30 September. Some have suggested that this was a significant event, signalling the beginning of the end for the Central Powers – perhaps a belated justification for the campaign as a whole. But as Trevor Wilson has pointed out, such an analysis is misleading. 'The German forces in France had been experiencing defeat for nearly two months before the Bulgarians acted on the awareness that the cause ... was truly lost.'[68]

* * *

As David French has written, 'the factor which dominated British strategy between 1914 and 1918 was that she fought the war as a member of a coalition'.[69] This had implications for every theatre in which British troops fought. But perhaps only in the Balkans did it mean making a major contribution to a military campaign which, according to the overwhelming majority of expert opinion, made no positive contribution towards winning the war. Indeed Robertson went so far as to suggest that Salonica was 'doing more to prevent us winning this war than anything else'.[70] In this light the comment of Salonica's official war correspondent that 'in every coalition something has to be sacrificed now and then to solidarity' seems something of an understatement.[71] Looking back on the war Edward Grey asserted that the first aim of allied diplomacy in wartime was to preserve solidarity. This was true enough. But the former Foreign Secretary could scarcely have had the Balkan expedition in mind when he concluded that this goal 'was completely and successfully achieved'.[72]

Notes

1. K. Halle, *Irrepressible Churchill: A Treasury of Winston Churchill's Wit* (Cleveland, 1966) p.157.
2. Sir J. Wheeler-Bennett, *King George VI: His Life and Reign* (London, 1958) p.460.
3. Ibid.
4. B. Pimlott (ed.), *The Second World War Diary of Hugh Dalton 1940-45* (London, 1986) p.694.
5. King's College, London, Liddell Hart Centre for Military Archives [hereafter LHCMA], Robertson MSS 1/22/84, Robertson to D. Haig 25 Oct. 1916.
6. Sir William Robertson, *Soldiers and Statesmen* (2 vols, London, 1926) vol.2, p.83.
7. G. Ward Price, *The Story of the Salonica Army* (London, 1918) p.237.
8. PRO, FO 371/2880/26310, Minute by Balfour on a memorandum by H. Nicolson on allied policy in Greece, 27 Jan. 1917.
9. PRO, CAB 37/136/4, Note by Lord Esher 12 Oct. 1915.
10. A. Pingaud, 'Les Origines de l'Expédition de Salonique', *Revue Historique* 176 (1935) p.449.
11. P. Azan, *Franchet d'Espérey* (Paris, 1949) pp.42-3.
12. Memorandum of 1 Jan. 1915, quoted in D.Lloyd George, *War Memoirs* (2 vols, London, 1938) vol.1, pp.219-26.
13. T. Wilson, *The Myriad Faces of War* (Oxford, 1986) p.105.
14. See G.H. Cassar, *The French and the Dardanelles* (London, 1971) pp.151-80; J. K. Tanenbaum, *General Maurice Sarrail 1856-1929* (Chapel Hill, 1974) pp.55-74.
15. ANP, Painlevé MSS, 313 Archives Privées 109, note (n.d.) by Colonel Bouët.
16. R. Poincaré, *Au Service de la France* (10 vols, Paris, 1926-33) vol.7, p.111.
17. MAE, 'Guerre', vol.283, J. Guillemin to Delcassé no.432, 19 Sept. 1915.
18. Ibid., no.440-1, 21 Sept. 1915.
19. Ibid., no.442, 21 Sept. 1915.

20. Ibid., no.443, Delcassé to Guillemin 23 Sept. 1915.
21. MAE 'Guerre', vol.1030, Military attaché, London, to Millerand 24 Sept. 1915.
22. Ibid., vol.283, Delcassé to Cambon no.3015, 23 Sept. 1915.
23. PRO, CAB 24/1/23, Note on the position in the Balkans 21 Sept. 1915.
24. Ibid., FO 371/2266/135856, Grey to Elliot 22 Sept. 1915.
25. Ibid., CAB 42/3/28, Dardanelles Committee 23 Sept. 1915.
26. Ibid., CAB 37/135/1, Asquith to George V 2 Oct. 1915.
27. Ibid., CAB 42/4/21.
28. Ibid., CAB 42/4/6, Summary of Joffre's note of 9 Oct. 1915.
29. MAE 'Guerre', vol.1030, Viviani to Cambon no.3307, 11 Oct. 1915; PRO, CAB 37/136/3, note by Grey.
30. R. Blake, *The Private Papers of Douglas Haig 1914-1919* (London, 1952) p.108.
31. MAE 'Guerre', vol.1031, Viviani to Cambon no.3403, 17 Oct. 1915.
32. PRO, CAB 37/136/17, Note from the Serbian legation 16 Oct. 1915.
33. LHCMA, Robertson MSS 1/8/26, Callwell to Robertson 20 Oct. 1915.
34. Ibid., 1/8/28, Callwell to Robertson 22 Oct. 1915.
35. Ibid., 1/8/29, Robertson to Callwell 23 Oct. 1915.
36. PRO, FO 371/2270/156928-9, Bertie to Grey 23 Oct. 1915.
37. Ibid., FO 371/2270/157600, Nicolson to Grey 24 Oct. 1915.
38. For Millerand's relationship with Joffre, see M. M. Farrar, 'Politics Versus Patriotism : Alexandre Millerand as French Minister of War', *French Historical Studies* 11 (1980) pp.577-609.
39. Cf. Sir Frederick Maurice, *Lessons of Allied Cooperation* (London, 1942) p.51.
40. PRO, CAB 42/4/17, Dardanelles Committee 25 Oct. 1915.
41. HLRO, Lloyd George MSS D/23/5/7, 'Views of the General Staff on the present situation at Salonica and in the Balkans with deductions as to our wisest course of action there' 23 Nov. 1915.
42. D.J. Dutton, 'The Calais Conference of December 1915', *Historical Journal* 21 (1978) pp.143-56.
43. S. Roskill, *Hankey: Man of Secrets* (3 vols, London, 1970-1974) vol.1, p.237.
44. V.H. Rothwell, *British War Aims and Peace Diplomacy 1914-1918* (Oxford, 1971) p.87; D. R. Woodward, *Lloyd George and the Generals* (London, 1983) p.113.
45. D.J. Dutton, 'The "Robertson Dictatorship" and the Balkan Campaign in 1916', *Journal of Strategic Studies* 9 (1986) pp.64-78.
46. Woodward, *Lloyd George* pp.76-7.
47. D.R. Woodward (ed.), *The Military Correspondence of Field-Marshal Sir*

William Robertson (London, 1989) pp.36-7.
48. J.M. Bourne, Britain and the Great War 1914-1918 (London, 1989) p.149.
49. HLRO, Lloyd George MSS E/5/1/3, A. Lee, 'Our Salonika-Balkan policy', 2 Dec. 1916.
50. LHCMA, Robertson MSS 1/32/9, Robertson to Murray 6 March 1916.
51. PRO, CAB 42/4/17, Dardanelles Committee 25 Oct. 1915.
52. Ibid., CAB 42/11/6, War Committee 21 March 1916.
53. Blake, Haig Papers p.137.
54. PRO, Bertie MSS, FO 800/172/Gr./16/38, Hardinge to Bertie 10 Oct. 1916.
55. Ibid., CAB 27/7/WP35, Memorandum by Lord Milner 8 July 1917.
56. LHCMA, Robertson MSS 1/14/48, Milne to Robertson 26 Oct. 1916.
57. PRO, Balfour MSS, FO 800/202, Milne to Robertson 28 Jan. 1917.
58. Ibid., CAB 24/6/GT84, Note by Balfour 27 Feb. 1917.
59. Ibid., FO 371/2865/60223, Memorandum by Mackenzie 5 March 1917.
60. C. Mackenzie, Greek Memories (London, 1939) p.75.
61. I have explored the reality of French ambitions in the Balkans in 'The Balkan Campaign and French War Aims in the Great War', English Historical Review 94 (1979) pp.97-113.
62. PRO, FO 371/2865/60223, Elliot to Mackenzie 7 March 1917.
63. Ibid., FO 371/2632/232768, Elliot to Grey 18 Nov. 1916.
64. Ibid., FO 371/2876/51525, Elliot to Balfour 9 March 1917.
65. HLRO, Lloyd George MSS F/55/3/2, Elliot to Hardinge 9 April 1917.
66. PRO, FO 371/2865/67185, Minutes on Bertie to Balfour 30 March 1917.
67. Ibid., FO 371/2878/83403, Draft of Cecil to Bertie April 1917.
68. Wilson, Myriad Faces p.620.
69. J. Turner (ed.), Britain and the First World War (London, 1988) p.24.
70. Woodward, Robertson Correspondence p.137.
71. Price, Salonica Army p.193.
72. Viscount Grey of Fallodon, Twenty-Five Years 1892-1916 (2 vols, London, 1925) vol.2, p.160.

Standard-bearers in a tangle: British perceptions of France after the First World War[1]

Alan Sharp

Marshal Foch was pessimistic from the outset. 'This is not a Peace, it is an Armistice for twenty years' was his judgement on the Treaty of Versailles.[1] Yet this gloomy verdict hardly seemed justified at the time. The democracies had triumphed and the extent of their victory was revealed in the German acceptance of the crippling terms of the armistice of 11 November 1918 leading to their signature of the peace treaty on 28 June 1919. With their main rivals defeated or incapacitated the post-war world seemed at their feet; none the less in 1939 Britain and France found themselves once again at war with Germany. Philip Bell has posed, in his elegant and masterly summary of the origins of the Second World War in Europe, the question as to how far two countries with so much in common had contributed to the very situation that both wished most anxiously to avoid, the renewal of hostilities on a large scale.[2] Why could the masters of Europe in 1918 not confound Foch and maintain European peace and stability for more than twenty years? Why did the standard-bearers of democracy get in such a tangle? This paper seeks to investigate British government and Foreign Office perceptions of France in the early post-war years in search of possible answers.[3]

That there was a strong and deeply rooted anti-French tradition in Britain is undeniable. As Robert Vansittart, a bastion of the inter-war Foreign Office, pointed out:

> the Victorian England in which I was brought up was almost entirely anti-French ... Victorian England was vaguely convinced that nineteenth-century France had too good a time; that France laughed too much and cooked too well for this vale of tears ... More serious still, Victorian England suspected that the French somehow put more into, and got more out of, sex than the English. Victorian England had not the vaguest idea how this was done, but was fairly sure that the advantage was not fair, and quite sure that it was not nice.

Paris in particular aroused British suspicion:

> the English always spoke of the place as 'Gay Parree' and were

profoundly unhappy when they got there ... I well remember how
... my great-aunt reproached my father when he first allowed me
to go to Paris as a boy. She said that I would return with no
morals and a Latin mind.

Despite the *Entente Cordiale* and the First World War itself there were
memories that went back for centuries and, like Lord Raglan during the
Crimean campaign, still some for whom 'the French' were synonymous with
'the enemy'.[4]

* * *

If the First World War began with Eyre Crowe in tears in sympathy for
France, it ended with suspicion.[5] As early as 2 December 1918 the future
Foreign Secretary, George Curzon, told the Eastern Committee, 'I am
seriously afraid that the great power from whom we have most to fear in
future is France'.[6] Curzon's main preoccupation was with France as an
imperial rival in the Middle and Near East but the peace conference reminded
British statesmen and public of European considerations and of traditional
quarrels and enmities. Robert Graves, up at Oxford after the war, recorded
that 'Anti-French feeling amongst most ex-soldiers amounted almost to an
obsession. Edmund [Blunden], shaking with nerves, used to say at this time:
"No more wars for me at any price! Except against the French. If there's
ever a war with them, I'll go like a shot." ... Some undergraduates even
insisted that we had been fighting on the wrong side: our natural enemies
were the French.'[7] Georges Clemenceau, the victorious French premier, after
receiving an Honorary Doctorate from the same University, declared to
Lloyd George in June 1921, 'I have to tell you that from the very day after
the Armistice I found you an enemy of France'. 'Well,' replied Lloyd
George, 'was it not always our traditional policy?'[8]

The review in March 1919 by Arthur Balfour, the British Foreign
Secretary, of the French arguments for an adjustment of their frontier with
Germany to give them a Rhineland buffer offers a more serious point of
departure. His perception of the post-war situation sums up many of the
points at issue between Great Britain and France in the 1920s and 1930s and
exposes many of the paradoxes at the heart of British decision-making, yet

it does so from a rather oblique angle, not always following the usual line taken by British observers. It reveals the common British exasperation with a France that refused to see matters from a British perspective. He did acknowledge that the French had some cause for concern, yet his overall assessment presaged the later frustration he so graphically expressed when he declared that they 'were so dreadfully afraid of being swallowed up by the tiger, but would spend their time poking it'.[9] There is thus an element of sympathy for France to be found in this assessment, mingled with annoyance that the French could not understand that their policies were creating (at least in Balfour's mind) precisely the dangers that they feared. Balfour wrote, 'They draw a lurid picture of future Franco-German relations. They assume that the German population will always far outnumber the French; that as soon as the first shock of defeat has passed away, Germany will organise herself for revenge; that all our attempts to limit armaments will be unsuccessful; that the League of Nations will be impotent; and consequently, that the invasion of France, which was accomplished in 1870, and partially accomplished in the recent War, will be renewed with every prospect of success.'[10] The historian can only acknowledge that these French fears were apparently confirmed by later events. But was this inevitable, was it the result of a British inability to assess accurately the real strengths of the continental powers or was it, as Balfour sought to warn in 1919, brought about by French attempts to disguise their underlying weakness by intransigence?

Thus far there was little unusual about his analysis, but Balfour continued,

I do not wish to deny the importance of these prophesyings: but I
do desire to point out that, in the first place, if there is a renewal
of German world politics, it is towards the East rather than
towards the West that her ambitions will probably be directed ...
If Germany is going again to be a great armed Camp, filled with
a population about twice as great as that of any other State in
Europe: and if she is going again to pursue a policy of world
domination, it will no doubt tax all the statesmanship of the rest of
the world to prevent a repetition of the calamities from which we
have been suffering. But the only radical cure for this is a change
in the international system of the world – a change which French
statesmen are doing nothing to promote, and the very possibility

of which many of them regard with ill concealed derision. They may be right; but if they are, it is quite certain that no manipulation of the Rhine frontier is going to make France anything more than a second-rate Power, trembling at the nod of its great neighbours on the East, and depending from day to day on the changes and chances of a shifting diplomacy and uncertain alliances.[11]

Balfour judged that France was now inescapably a second-rate power. Yet many of Britain's problems of policy arose because she was caught between this assessment and its paradoxical alternative, that France was not only a great power but *the* great power most likely to be Britain's main opponent in the post-war world. In one sense the population and industrial production figures did show France to be on the very margin of the requirements of great power status,[12] but she had just fought and won a massive war and she was clearly a major actor in a world where so many of the traditional authorities had collapsed, however artificial that post-war international balance might be. Thus France had to be treated like a great power and accorded the respect due to one, but this was not easy to reconcile with the apparent lack of French self-confidence revealed by requests for a British alliance and an unwillingness (as Britain saw it) to show any generosity towards Germany. Britain was irritated that France expected Britain to commit herself in an unprecedented manner to European politics but showed no inclination in return to follow a British lead in world affairs. At almost every turn the two main European allies in the recent conflict found their paths crossing and it was clear that each had a very different perspective and agenda. Yet much as each might have wished to act independently of the other, the reality was that neither could do so successfully because each could frustrate and thwart the other's initiatives.

Balfour's memorandum is also significant because it recognised Eastern Europe as the most likely point of tension in the post-war continent though few, if any, of his colleagues were prepared to follow this judgement, and British policy was certainly not founded upon this premise, something that the French found both frustrating and naive. Furthermore most of his contemporaries believed that Germany no longer represented the most pressing threat to the European balance of power (a concept still widely valued in post-war British decision-making circles despite its political incorrectness in a Wilsonian world). Balfour's analysis acknowledged Germany as a potential disturber of the peace, an interesting if somewhat unorthodox assessment of the European situation, but one which did recognise the triangular relationship between France, Germany and Great Britain to be at the heart of European politics.

The British elite were suspicious of France because they perceived her to be ambitious, to have the means to translate those ambitions into reality and to be without a genuine continental rival. Lord D'Abernon, the first British post-war ambassador to Germany, wrote in 1923, 'Many of the arguments which were valid in 1914 against Germany are valid today against France ... Anyone who supposes that a French Government dominating the Continent as Napoleon dominated it after Tilsit will remain friendly to England must be a poor judge of national psychology ... Desiring the maintenance of the Anglo-French Entente, I am compelled to desire the existence of a strong Germany.'[13] Britain judged that the French had the largest army in the world and feared that their submarine and military aircraft production plans were drawn up, partly at least, with Britain in mind. At the same time there was some recognition that France did have genuine concerns about her future security but this tended to be obscured by other explanations of her behaviour and policies. As Robert Vansittart succinctly put it, with belated insight: 'We all blamed France ... for being vindictive, when her real motive was funk.'[14]

Britain's suspicions of France were based upon economic and territorial considerations in Europe and upon imperial rivalries elsewhere. Curzon told the assembled delegates to the Imperial Conference in London in June 1921:

> There has never disappeared from her imagination the lure of the Ruhr Valley, and one of the objects for which we here, and especially the Prime Minister, have successfully struggled, has been to prevent her from carrying out this occupation of German territory which her military advisers have always had in view. The Ministers present will see at once what her object is – with Lorraine, the Saar Valley and the Ruhr in her occupation, she becomes the mistress of Europe in respect of coal, iron and steel, and with those countries under her military command she would also become the military monarch. Those quite frankly are the

ambitions lurking, I will not say in the minds of the French Government, but of a large section of French opinion, with which we are confronted.[15]

This suspicion was encouraged by the almost inevitable French demand that each and every German infraction of the Treaty should be punished by an occupation of the Ruhr. Captain Georgi, a British adviser on coal and steel matters, offered an interesting economic explanation of the 'lure of the Ruhr' whose occupation was: 'inevitable not because they, the French, by doing so wish to cripple Germany, this latter consideration is really to my mind a subsidiary one, but because present schemes of industrialising France on a large scale can only assume a concrete form if the Ruhr, wholly or partly comes under French control ...'. As Sidney Waterlow, a clerk in the Foreign Office Central Department, commented on 25 November 1920, 'If he is right ... we cannot expect the danger to diminish with the return of political tranquillity or the lapse of time'.[16] Although Lloyd George did acquiesce in an actual extension of the occupied area of Germany in March 1921 and agreed to the threat of a further extension in April 1921, thus making it more difficult for Britain to protest when the French, in association with the Belgians, occupied the whole of the Ruhr in 1923,[17] the more usual British reaction was to resist such demands. As Curzon declared: 'We are at the present moment ... the only moderating influence in respect of France. We go about arm in arm with her, but with one of our hands on her collar, and if we relax that control I myself should be very much alarmed at the consequences that would ensue.'[18] Even when Lloyd George did accept the extended occupation of March 1921 he emphasised so much the need for France to disavow any annexationist objectives in the Rhineland that the French premier, Aristide Briand, asked, 'if, in the composition of a Welshman, there was not a little bit of a Norman, i.e., a *soupçon* of mistrust!'.[19]

*   *   *

The belief that the French had designs on German territory was never far from the minds of many British diplomats in the immediate post-war era and, quite apart from the frequent demands for the occupation of the Ruhr, they found evidence to support their views in various French policies and initiatives at all levels of seriousness. The major criticism of the Treaty in France was that it had not dismembered the German empire. There had been a formidable French campaign during the Paris peace conference to detach the Rhineland from Germany and to obtain the Saar in absolute sovereignty, in short to reverse the provisions of the 1815 peace settlement in this area. Foch had been tireless in advocating a French military, if not political, frontier on the Rhine and British observers did not believe that this policy had been abandoned with the signing of the Treaty.[20] They saw confirmation of this judgement in the French attempts to get the Rhineland High Commission, the body responsible for overseeing the occupied zones of Germany, to take over the administration of food supplies for the region. Harold Stuart, the British Commissioner, pointed out: 'If the Allies take over the food administration ... it will be necessary to take over financial administration also in order to obtain the funds required to pay for the food stuffs, which it would be necessary to import; and that would be used as an argument for taking over the Ruhr basin, which is so closely connected economically with the occupied territories'. He suspected a well coordinated French policy aimed at Rhenish separatism and an occupation of the Ruhr. Lord Hardinge, the Permanent Under-Secretary at the Foreign Office, commented, 'The French are determined to get Rhineland [sic]'.[21] French insistence that the railways in the occupied area should conform to Western European, rather than Central European, time in the winter months, when the French reverted to the former, was seen as a further indication – 'a fondness for anything that links up the occupied territory with France rather than with unoccupied Germany'.[22] French pressure for separate diplomatic representation in the various constituent states of Germany, especially Saxony and Bavaria, was seen as an attempt to foster separatism in the hope of encouraging the secession of catholic South Germany from the protestant North, though one view in the Foreign Office was that it was counter-productive: 'If only the French abstain from "encouraging" it the separatist movement in the South may well materialise'.[23]

The most serious incident in Anglo-French relations before the Ruhr occupation of 1923 was the unilateral occupation by the French of Frankfurt, Darmstadt and three other German towns on 5/6 April 1920 in the confused aftermath of the Kapp *putsch* of 13 March. Kapp's attempted right-wing coup against the legitimate government in Berlin had collapsed within four days but the resulting disorder in Germany, and particularly in the Ruhr, revealed serious differences between the two allies. First the Kapp government and then the legal government requested permission to send extra troops into the demilitarised area of the Rhineland in order to suppress alleged communist uprisings. Whilst the British government was, perhaps over-hastily, prepared to accept the official German request as justified, the French were determined that either the allies should themselves intervene to restore order or that they would consent to the German reinforcements only if French troops were allowed to occupy another part of the Ruhr. This created instant suspicion in the Foreign Office. Waterlow commented, to general approval, 'The French Government are evidently working to use the situation as a pretext for occupying the Ruhr basin and detaching the Rhineland'.[24] After much confusion the French, against the declared wishes of their main ally, acted alone and carried out the occupation of the five towns in the name of the allies. The Conservative leader, Andrew Bonar Law, who had interviewed the French ambassador, Paul Cambon, in Lloyd George's absence, wrote to the prime minister, 'You will I am sure feel so angry about this that if we were talking my desire would be to rather put whatever little curb I could upon your feelings than to stimulate them, but I do not think this can be left where it is'.[25] The British reaction was measured but firm. Curzon had already suggested that such action might lead to a British withdrawal from the Rhineland occupation,[26] but the immediate response was less dramatic – Derby was withdrawn from the Ambassadors' Conference in Paris. Crowe's view was that Britain could either use the episode as the occasion of a complete breach with the French, an 'heroic solution' which he rejected, or she could treat the crisis as 'a lover's quarrel' and try to create better relations with France, a policy that he favoured because of the many problems that could only be solved by Anglo-French cooperation. Hence he thought Britain should attempt 'to build golden bridges for the retirement of the French from their present false position'. Curzon was less sympathetic, despite his appreciation of the motives behind Crowe's advice: 'After so flagrant a case as this, however, I am not very enthusiastic about "kissing again with tears".'[27] The British left their allies in no doubt as to the serious view they took of unilateral action and, although the incident was smoothed over when Millerand agreed to promise that France would not again act without the consent of her allies, it left a bitter aftertaste.[28]

Once again the French seemed to be fulfilling the role that the British feared. At the peace conference one of the most vivid images that Lloyd George evoked was of the statue of Strasbourg in the Place de la Concorde veiled in mourning in memory of the lost provinces of Alsace-Lorraine.[29] He expressed frequently his fear of creating a mirror image of the 1871 situation, the nightmare of Alsace-Lorraine in reverse, and this metaphor was never far from his mind in the post-war period. British opinion accepted that at least part of the French motivation in seeking to detach the Rhineland (and other parts of Germany) lay in her need for security. The question was how Britain should respond and opinion amongst those who accepted some European responsibilities was divided between those who argued that a more secure France would be more amenable and generous and those who believed that the more uncertain France was of British support, the easier it would be to keep her in check. Lloyd George's imaginative, but probably insincere, offer of a guarantee to France in March 1919, provided she would renounce her schemes to detach the Rhineland from Germany, established a new theme in Anglo-French relations, the idea that wartime cooperation might be continued by a formal pact in peacetime. This was such a burning ambition of Clemenceau's that, although he did undoubtedly obtain further important concessions before conceding the Rhineland plans, he was probably over-anxious to clinch the deal and was effectively hoodwinked by Lloyd George's eleventh-hour linkage of the operation of the British guarantee to the separate American pact.[30] At all events Britain had secured her objective without paying the agreed price, though some recognised that a moral obligation did persist. The post-war discussions about a guarantee, or, as the French preferred, an alliance, reveal much about the attitudes and beliefs of the British decision-making elite. There were some, like Lloyd George's private secretary, Philip Kerr, who advised withdrawal from European affairs: 'Ever since the loss by the British Crown of its French possessions it has been a fundamental instinct with the British people to avoid intervention in Europe except in crises which threatened their own security. I believe this instinct is a sound one and I feel convinced that the feeling will rapidly grow in

England that we have so many problems of our own at home, that we had better leave Europe to itself with such assistance as the League of Nations can give to it.' Kerr advised Lloyd George to 'draw in our horns in Foreign Affairs ... [and] turn your whole attention to the problems of Great Britain and the British Empire'.[31] He was supported by the influential South African, Jan Christian Smuts, who advised a policy of Imperial isolation: 'I would rather assume a position of independence, putting the British Empire entirely aside from all of them', but the same delegates at the Imperial Conference in London in 1921 were graphically reminded by Winston Churchill of the difficulties of such a stance: 'There are thousands of graves in France ...'.[32]

* * *

It was too late to argue that Britain could absolve herself of all responsibilities for European affairs and her freedom of choice in the post-war world was much restricted by the choice she had made in 1914, but those who advocated a firm commitment to a French alliance were just as much in a minority as were the out-and-out isolationists. Lord Derby, the British Ambassador in Paris, 1918-1920, and later War Minister under Bonar Law in 1922, was a convinced francophile and believer in the need for a close and formal relationship. His letter to Lloyd George of 10 June 1921 is interesting because it highlights the important difference of perspective between the British, who saw Germany as a nation of 65 million customers, and the French perception of a powerful nation in arms:

> Living as I do in the greatest commercial district of England I am extremely anxious to see good commercial relationships existing between our country and Germany, but I feel that just as I would like to see Germany re-established as a commercial nation, so must the French nation feel that if she is so re-established that there may be a danger of her again reconstructing her Army and Navy and attempting a War of revenge ... the question is how can these views be so reconciled as to give us the commercial intercourse with Germany which we desire and at the same time safeguard France from military aggression.

Derby argued that an alliance would both offer the French security and 'as partners we should have a right ... to warn the other, if it was thought that the policy that was being pursued was not conducive to peace'. Austen Chamberlain, after 1921 the Conservative leader in the Lloyd George coalition, also argued that the best way for Britain to achieve her objectives in western Europe lay in an alliance: 'if it be once admitted that we cannot afford to see Germany dominating Belgium and Holland or overwhelming France, is it not far better that this vital object of British policy should be consecrated and defended by a public treaty...?' The Chief of the Imperial General Staff, Sir Henry Wilson, was even more committed: 'I conclude that a close offensive and defensive Alliance should be entered into between the British, French and Belgian Governments', whilst Churchill believed that an alliance was necessary to encourage a more positive French attitude to the problems of the post-war world. Charles Hardinge, Derby's successor in Paris, shared this view: 'I feel that until France obtains some guarantee of assistance by us against possible aggression by Germany, she will continue to be unreasonable and tiresome over all questions affecting her relations with Germany'.[33]

The Labour Party, the main opposition in the House of Commons, took a different line. Its leader, Arthur Henderson, wrote to Lloyd George on 7 January 1920, 'we hold most decidedly that a commitment of this kind is unnecessary, since the Covenant of the League of Nations imposes already the obligation to defend the territorial integrity and independence of all its members. Further, although this alliance may be in form defensive, it must have the effect of diminishing the motives which would otherwise incline French policy to courses of prudence and conciliation'.[34] Whilst many British observers would have recognised the first argument, however logical, to be unrealistic, the second certainly struck a chord. It was readily accepted and developed by someone who had little sympathy with any policy linking British fortunes to the Continent, Sir Maurice Hankey,[35] the Secretary to the Cabinet, an office whose responsibilities he was largely defining by his own endeavours.

> If France is unlikely to accept our lead on the outstanding questions in return for the guarantee, our experience of the past does not lead us to think that she would be more tractable after a guarantee had been given. The guarantee to France was signed at

the end of June, 1919. After that date the French Government was
in fact no easier to deal with than it was before ... In fact, it is not
unlikely that France would be more pugnacious than ever. We
should constantly be in the dilemma of having to choose between
breaking off the Alliance and associating ourselves in a policy
utterly distasteful to us and liable to lead to a breach of the
peace.[36]

The crux of Hankey's argument was, however, more crudely expressed:
'it is doubtful if France could be bought, and even if she were bought it is
doubtful if she would stay bought'.[37] This was, for many, the key point.
Crowe commented, in June 1921,

> I believe they want the alliance against Germany. But when it
> comes to dropping anti-British policy in the rest of the world,
> France, true to her traditional practice, wants to sell her support
> in each field in return for separate rewards. In other words she
> would claim our support against Germany as something to be
> given in any case, and for nothing. But French support for British
> policy in the East or elsewhere is something for which England
> must pay by special and valuable concessions. Much as I am in
> favour of a comprehensive understanding with France, to which
> Great Britain would contribute in the shape of an alliance against
> German unprovoked aggression, I should hesitate to recommend
> it on such terms.

Although the French might legitimately have objected that, given the
Rhineland negotiations of March 1919, it was the British who expected to be
paid twice for the same horse, there can be no doubt that Crowe spoke for
most uncommitted British decision-makers, not least the Foreign Secretary,
who declared in December 1921, 'I earnestly hope that it will not be
proposed to give the guarantee for nothing'. Hardinge agreed: Curzon should
certainly press for concessions from the French over their submarine building
programme and over Tangiers; in return Britain should offer assistance over
reparations and German disarmament, 'but there should be no concession on
our part of any kind without an entire change of attitude on the part of the
French'.[38]

Curzon's long discussion of the possibilities of an Anglo-French alliance is revealing on another count. It is clear that Curzon recognised the European advantages of such an arrangement but that he doubted its world-wide and imperial value and that these were the considerations that weighed more heavily with him.[39] The instinctive British desire to remain as uncommitted to European affairs as possible which had been implicit in Lloyd George's Fontainebleau Memorandum remained powerful both in this paper and in the negotiations about the possibility of building a Channel Tunnel which revealed many of the establishment's unspoken assumptions. 'It may of course be said', wrote Balfour in his contribution to the debate, 'that the unknown dangers which I fear may possibly be of a kind which will put an end to our position as an island Power, and make the command of the sea useless as a means of defence. It may be so; but let us wait till it is so, and as long as the ocean remains our friend do not let us deliberately destroy its power to help us.' J.M. Keynes, who considered himself a European as well as an Englishman, asserted in 1919, 'England still stands outside Europe. Europe's voiceless tremors do not reach her. Europe is apart and England is not part of her flesh and body.' Fog in the Channel still meant that the Continent was isolated! Indeed as late as 1930 a distinguished ex-Foreign Secretary, Austen Chamberlain, considered it worth his while to read to such an informed body as the Royal Institute of International Affairs a paper entitled 'Great Britain as a European Power'. There was, apparently, still some doubt on the subject.[40]

* * *

It was precisely because there was this ambiguity as to Britain's perception of her own role and world position that many of the problems with France arose. Britain wanted a France confident enough to be generous to Germany but sufficiently unsure of herself to accept a British lead — yet it appeared that the only way in which the French could display independence and confidence was in rejecting British policies and asserting her own, thus in British eyes both exacerbating the original problems and justifying British reluctance to assist her. Britain wished to avoid continental commitment but France could only be reassured by a Britain that was committed to a strong European role. There was a further complication. The French definition of continental commitment far outstripped anything that even those in Britain sympathetic to her cause could accept. Whilst Austen Chamberlain, for example, could see a direct British interest in the security of France and the Low Countries, he did not accept the persistent French assertion that a new German offensive would turn east before it attempted to deal with western Europe — the French shorthand was that there would be a new Sadowa before any new Sedan. Thus, despite the efforts of James Headlam-Morley, the Historical Adviser to the Foreign Office, there was no positive British response to the French request for guarantees for the new states of eastern Europe without which, the French argued, any British pact with France would be of very limited value. Headlam-Morley knew what the practical objections to such a policy were, but he was increasingly persuaded that Britain's self-interest demanded a greater awareness of eastern European affairs. Most of his colleagues remained unconvinced. He is, none the less, an interesting example of a decision-maker who modified his views about France after 1919 from suspicion to sympathetic understanding.[41]

Personalities had, perhaps, some part to play. The British found Aristide Briand a more congenial partner than Raymond Poincaré, about whom few could find a good word to say. Briand, the Breton, and Lloyd George, the Welshman, could at least find consolation in memories of a common enmity against the English, but Poincaré was, according to Hardinge, 'a dirty dog, a man of very mean character'. Curzon agreed: 'How tired I am of this eternal crisis with France and I wish Poincaré with his meticulous hostility was at the bottom of the sea for ever'.[42] The double-edged sword of secret intelligence did not always assist Curzon's equanimity; he was distraught at the intrigue between Poincaré and the French ambassador in London, the Comte de St Aulaire, revealed by intercepted and decrypted French telegrams in October 1923. 'This is the worst thing I have come across in my public life and it will render it absolutely impossible for me ever to treat St Aulaire with the slightest confidence again', he complained to Lord Crewe, the British ambassador in Paris.[43] Set against this, Lloyd George's reputation in Paris (or indeed anywhere else) as a man of his word was not high,[44] but these considerations were not at the heart of the problem.

The key question was whether the two allies could overcome their mutual suspicions and the difficulties engendered by their different geographical perspectives and their perceptions of 'the lessons of history'. It was certainly not clear to the participants in the immediate aftermath of a victorious war that the era of European hegemony was waning fast and that they could not afford the luxury of a debilitating struggle for an illusory supremacy. It might be argued that the French did begin, dimly, to grasp this but, paradoxically, could see no other way in which to assert their aspirations to remain a great power other than to engage in competition with the British. Yet almost every post-war problem had an Anglo-French dimension – inter-allied debts, the Middle, Near and Far East, and colonial issues around the globe, but above all else the dilemmas that surrounded the execution of the treaty with Germany and their mutually incompatible visions of the appropriate place and role for Germany in the post-war world. Any satisfactory and lasting solution to any of these matters would require a close Anglo-French understanding and hence it was deeply significant that Hardinge could write in 1920 that 'our relations with France never have been, are not and probably never will be sufficiently stable and friendly to justify the construction of a Channel Tunnel'.[45] Five years later the French ambassador in London, Aimé-Joseph de Fleuriau, was convinced that the battle for British hearts and minds was all but lost:

> No more commitments in foreign policy. This will dominate British thinking more and more and we are seeing the same trends as a century ago but accentuated by the fact that the oligarchy of 1820 has become the democracy of 1925. Talented writers cannot convince the British people that the Rhine is their frontier. Very few can understand that their frontier is not the sea and their number will scarcely be increased as a result of what they are taught in school. What does still exist and may persist is a feeling of friendliness based on memories of the war but we shall certainly be unable to convince the English of the need to stand by us if we try to appeal to their self-interest.[46]

Thus the two allies had failed to develop a unity of purpose in the post-war world, indeed for both it was almost as if there was some consolation in the comforting familiarity of Anglo-French rivalry in a world of alarming and extraordinary change; the standard bearers of democracy were already in a tangle.

Notes

I am indebted to the Librarians and Archivists of the Universities of Ulster and Cambridge, the Public Record Office, the House of Lords Record Office, the British Library and the Quai d'Orsay.

1. W.S. Churchill, *The Gathering Storm* (London, 1949 edn.) p.6.
2. P.M.H. Bell, *The Origins of the Second World War in Europe* (London, 1986) p.89.
3. There are some fascinating insights about wider British attitudes in John C. Cairns, 'A Nation of Shopkeepers in Search of a Suitable France: 1919-1949', *American Historical Review* 79 (1974) pp.710-43.
4. Robert Vansittart, *Lessons of My Life* (London, [?1943]) pp.21-2; A. Wood, *Nineteenth Century Britain 1815-1914* (London, 1960) p.194.
5. Vansittart recorded that 'Going to Crowe's room for an outlet of pent emotions, I found the dry man dissolved; tears glistened down the furrows of his face, and all that he could say was "the poor French"...': Robert Vansittart, *The Mist Procession* (London, 1958) p.127.
6. PRO, CAB 24/27, Eastern Committee minutes.
7. R. Graves, *Goodbye to All That* (Penguin edn., Harmondsworth, 1963) p.240.
8. G. Clemenceau, *Grandeur and Misery of Victory* (London, 1930) p.113. See also J. B. Duroselle, *Clemenceau* (Paris, 1988) p.879.
9. PRO, CAB 24/172/4651, Committee of Imperial Defence meeting 13 Feb. 1925.
10. BL, Balfour Papers, Add MS 49751, Balfour Memorandum 18 March 1919.
11. Ibid.
12. P. Kennedy, *The Rise and Fall of the Great Powers: Economic Change and Military Conflict from 1500 to 2000* (Paperback edn, London, 1989) pp.355-430; P. Bernard and H. Dubief, *The Decline of the Third Republic 1914-1938* (Cambridge, 1988) pp.102-47; Bell, *Origins* pp.90-100.
13. Lord D'Abernon, *An Ambassador of Peace* (3 vols, London, 1929) vol.2, pp.238-9.
14. Vansittart, *Mist Procession* p.206.
15. PRO, CAB 32/2/E4, Meeting 22 June 1921.
16. Ibid., FO 371/4775, C12185/192/18, Paper by Georgi and minute by Waterlow, both 25 Nov. 1920.
17. See the helpful summary in S. Crowe and E. Corp, *Our Ablest Public Servant: Sir Eyre Crowe 1864-1925* (Braunton, 1993) pp.430-3.

18. PRO, CAB 32/2/E4, Meeting 22 June 1921.
19. Inter-Allied Conference, London, 9 March 1921, ICP 182: E.L. Woodward, R. Butler et al., *Documents on British Foreign Policy 1919-1939, First Series* (27 vols, London, 1947-1986) [hereafter *DBFP*] vol.15, pp.356-8.
20. See J.C. King, *Foch versus Clemenceau: France and German Dismemberment, 1918-1919* (Harvard, 1960) pp.73-112; R. McCrum, 'French Rhineland Policy at the Paris Peace Conference, 1919', *Historical Journal* 21 (1978) pp.623-48.
21. Stuart unnumbered despatch 16 Feb. 1920, *DBFP*, vol.9, p.71 and p.71 n.3.
22. PRO, FO 371/4266, C9162/6454/18, J. Cooper minute 21 Oct. 1920 (file 6454 covers the railway issue).
23. See PRO, FO 371/4266, 180684/7067/39, Lord Derby (Paris) despatch 531, 23 Feb. 1920; FO 371/3793, Director of Military Intelligence to FO 25 Aug. 1919; FO 371/3783, 191695/4232/18, Eric Phipps minute, April 1920.
24. See the British statements by Curzon and Lloyd George at the Inter-Allied Conference, 18 March 1920, ICP 78: *DBFP,* vol.8, pp.542, 547 (Derby (Paris) tel 301, 16 March 1920, gave the French reaction: ibid., vol.9, pp.150-1); PRO, FO 371/3780, 185720/4232/18, Waterlow's minute 16 March 1920.
25. HLRO, Lloyd George MSS, F/3/1/31, Bonar Law to Lloyd George 6 April 1920.
26. FO tel 401, 1 April 1920: *DBFP*, vol.9, p.282. Curzon had considerably strengthened the original draft, see PRO, FO 371/3781, 189367/4232/18.
27. Crowe memorandum and Curzon's minute 6 April 1920: *DBFP*, vol.9, pp.327-8 and p.328, n.1.
28. Derby tel 458, 11 April 1920: ibid., p.383.
29. P. Mantoux and André Tardieu record Lloyd George using almost identical words on separate occasions: P. Mantoux, *Paris Peace Conference 1919: Proceedings of the Council of Four, March 24 - April 18* (Geneva, 1964) p.28; A. Tardieu, *The Truth about the Treaty* (London, 1921) p.171.
30. This episode is thoroughly investigated in A. Lentin, 'The Treaty That Never Was: Lloyd George and the abortive Anglo-French Alliance of 1919' in J. Loades (ed.), *The Life and Times of David Lloyd George* (Bangor, 1991) pp.115-28.
31. HLRO, Lloyd George MSS, F/90/1/18, Memorandum 2 Sept. 1920.
32. PRO, CAB 32/2/E6, Smuts, 24 June 1921; CAB 32/2/E7, Churchill, 27 June 1921.
33. HLRO, Lloyd George MSS, F/14/5/27, Derby to Lloyd George 10 June 1921, quoted by R. S. Churchill, *Lord Derby: King of Lancashire* (London, 1959) pp.397-8; PRO, CAB 4/7, C.I.D. Paper 246-B, Chamberlain, 28 June 1920; CAB 24/101, CP 919, Wilson, 20 March 1920; CAB 23/25, Cabinet 40 (20)

Conclusion 4, Churchill, 24 May 1921; HLRO, Lloyd George MSS, F/53/1/63, Hardinge, private letter to Lloyd George, 22 June 1921.

34. HLRO, Lloyd George MSS, F/27/3/39.

35. Hankey opposed the idea of a Channel tunnel with particular assiduity over several administrations and he did not want Britain to guarantee the Franco-German frontier or to become involved in eastern Europe. See S. Roskill, *Hankey: Man of Secrets* (3 vols, London, 1970-1974) vol.2, passim.

36. HLRO, Lloyd George MSS, F/25/1/48, Hankey to Lloyd George 25 June 1921.

37. Ibid.

38. PRO, FO 371/6995, W6298/6298/17, Crowe minute 14 June 1921 (Curzon added 'Or at this time' 15 June 1921); Curzon memorandum 28 Dec. 1921: *DBFP* vol.16, p.869; CUL, Hardinge Papers vol.45, Hardinge to Curzon 3 Jan. 1922.

39. *DBFP* vol.16, pp.860-70.

40. PRO, FO 371/3765, C.I.D Paper 96-A, 5 Feb. 1920 (for a fuller discussion of this issue see A. Sharp, 'Britain and the Channel Tunnel 1919-1920', *Australian Journal of Politics and History* 25 (1979) pp.210-15); J.M. Keynes, *The Economic Consequences of the Peace* (London, 1919, references here to the American edn., 1920) pp.2, 8; Austen Chamberlain, 'Great Britain as a European Power', *Journal of the Royal Institute of International Affairs* (1930) vol.9, pp.180-8.

41. For his early suspicions, see his minute of 16 Jan. 1919 on the General Staff Memorandum on the future Franco-German frontier (PRO, FO 371/4377). See also his paper on the Guarantee Treaties of 17 Jan. 1922 (FO 371/8286): 'We can, as is proposed, give a guarantee against German aggression on the Rhine or through Belgium. But more probably the real danger in the future may lie rather on the eastern frontiers of Germany – Danzig, Poland and Czechoslovakia – for it is in these districts that the settlement of Paris would be, when the time came, most easily overthrown. But in these districts no military help would be available from this country, and this is one reason why it is impossible now to satisfy the demands of our French allies.' See also his prescient memorandum on 'British Policy and the Geneva Protocol' (12 Feb. 1925). 'Has anyone attempted to realise what would happen if there were to be a new partition of Poland, or if the Czechoslovak State was to be so curtailed and dismembered that in fact it disappeared from the map of Europe? ... Imagine ... that Austria rejoined Germany; that Germany using the discontented minority in Bohemia demanded a new frontier far over the mountains including Carlsbad and Pilsen, and at the same time, in alliance with Germany, the Hungarians recovered the southern slope of the Carpathians. This would be

catastrophic, and, even if we neglected to interfere to prevent it happening, we should be driven to interfere, probably too late.' Chamberlain commented, 'I would say broadly that in Western Europe we are a partner; that, comparatively speaking, in Eastern Europe our role should rather be that of a disinterested *amicus curiae* ...' (PRO, FO 371/11064, W1252/9/98, Headlam-Morley's memorandum and Chamberlain's comments 21 Feb. 1925). The memorandum is reprinted in Sir J. W. Headlam-Morley, *Studies in Diplomatic History* (London, 1930) pp.171-92.

42. G. Tabouis, *Perfidious Albion - Entente Cordiale* (London, 1938) p.1; CUL, Hardinge Papers vol.48, Hardinge to Curzon 5 May 1922, and Curzon to Hardinge 8 May 1922.

43. CUL, Crewe MSS C/12, Curzon to Crewe 13 Oct. 1923. See also K. Jeffery and A. Sharp, 'Lord Curzon and Secret Intelligence' in C. Andrew and J. Noakes (eds), *Intelligence and International Relations 1900-1945* (Exeter, 1987) pp.103-26.

44. See A. Sharp, 'Lloyd George and Foreign Policy, 1918-1922: The "And Yet" Factor' in Loades (ed.), *Lloyd George* pp.129-42.

45. PRO, FO 371/3765, 187042/183192/17, Hardinge memorandum, no date but written between 7 April 1920 and 1 May 1920.

46. MAE, Europe 1918-29, File GB 80, De Fleuriau to Laroche, private letter 23 July 1925.

'Through a glass, darkly'
The Foreign Office investigation
of French federalism, January-May 1930

Ralph White

At the League of Nations Assembly in September 1929 the French Foreign Minister, Aristide Briand, famously declared his interest in the principle of a federal Europe.[1] He undertook to submit a memorandum on the subject to European member governments to elicit their views. At the end of 1929 the Foreign Office finally convinced itself that Briand's federalist utterances required serious attention. In the event of a French governmental initiative, British officials felt they should be prepared – but for what? That was the problem.

Early in January 1930 officials grasped the nettle: they concluded that the implications of French federalist talk had to be divined, months before Briand presented his memorandum on European Federal Union on 17 May. This did not reflect any increase in sympathy for Europeanist proposals, any latter-day conversion; rather, it was a victory for those realists who sensed that such proposals could be important insofar as the French deemed them so, at the expense of those sceptics who were preoccupied with their implausibility.

The attempt to decode what Briand and others meant by their increased references to 'organising' or 'federalising' Europe quickly threw up possibilities that officials found new and, in some respects, alarming. For in the course of this exercise French federalist ideas were located in three further and related contexts to complement that of intercontinental economic bargaining and tariff policy in which these same ideas were viewed in 1929. The contexts were first, that of French political and economic policy objectives in Europe; second, that of Franco-German rapprochement; and third, that of the emergence of a new era in European affairs, and with this, of a new European order, consequent upon what was called 'the liquidation of the war'.

Suddenly, in the early weeks of 1930, Foreign Office staff were jolted out of their habitual complacency about Europeanism. They tumbled to the possibility of a united Europe emerging at France's behest and under Franco-German hegemony, excluding Great Britain and profoundly inimical to British interests. Officials were worried, and the realists unhappily vindicated, until this possibility was scotched as a result of urgent and extensive consultations in Berlin and Rome, as well as Paris. The more disturbing scenarios from a Foreign Office point of view were set aside; they were replaced in late spring by a bemused and mildly apprehensive anticipation of Briand's specific proposals. In any case one result of this New Year reconnaissance was clear: Europeanism had ceased to be a laughing matter.

* * *

The pacemaker was the Paris embassy under Lord Tyrrell. In a number of despatches covering the debates in the Chamber of Deputies in November and December 1929 Tyrrell emphasized the importance of the references both to Franco-German rapprochement and to France's need to organise or federalise Europe. On 1 January Howard Smith, head of the Western department, minuted on the latest of these despatches:

> We shall have to make up our minds exactly what M. Briand is after and whether his proposals would suit the British Empire. So far I do not think that much attention has been paid to his declaration at Geneva.[2]

Sargent, head of the Central department, seized on a fresh dimension and exposed his own view of European federalism:

> I notice that on this occasion M. Herriot and M. Briand also dragged in the Protocol. This is quite a different proposition to that of the United States of Europe and we ought to be careful to keep them quite distinct - the one aims at affording security against military aggression; the other at establishing a system of economic cooperation.[3]

The upshot was a letter to Chapman, Permanent Under Secretary at the Board of Trade, enquiring whether the Board was studying the federal Europe idea and emphasising the disquiet of the Foreign Office at the apparent linking of this with the Geneva Protocol.[4]

A few days later another communication from Tyrrell provoked the next move. He quoted an inspired report in *Le Temps* asserting that the French government was sympathetic to Polish-German understanding, and stressed also the government's willingness to do everything possible to bring Germany into 'the Europe which France is organising', and which must be based on Franco-German cooperation.[5] This incited E.H. Carr, Second Secretary in the Central section, to a withering riposte:

> I am driven to the conclusion that hot air is as predominant an element in this Franco-German talk as it was in M. Briand's pan-European claptrap at Geneva ... I should, at any rate, like to see evidence, other than talk, to indicate that it should be taken seriously. The Germans, to my mind, estimate its value quite correctly, and have taken no notice of it whatever.[6]

Howard Smith, although conceding that the whole pan-European idea was 'very nebulous at present', thought that Briand might produce some scheme of economic cooperation plus non-aggression before September. 'It may be very awkward for us', he wrote, and proposed that Tyrrell be asked to explain just what he meant by the expression 'the Europe which France is organising'. Vansittart, the new Permanent Under Secretary, agreed, though doubting that much would then come of the enquiry.[7] The result was a letter from Arthur Henderson, Foreign Secretary, to Tyrrell on 18 January seeking clarification of recent French utterances on this 'somewhat nebulous and very complicated question'. Henderson's apprehension was obvious, based as it was on his officials' fear that the French might be combining political and economic dimensions in their federalism:

> It seems, therefore, that certain politicians in France, if not M. Briand himself, are considering a scheme of combining Europe in some kind of organisation bound together by a system of economic cooperation and agreement for non-aggression. Whether or not such a plan is practical politics at the present moment, it seems to me that it might be fraught with certain dangers for this country, and that the two questions of economic cooperation and security against military aggression should be kept distinct.[8]

The enquiry to the Board of Trade produced an unenlightening response from Chapman at the end of January: 'It seems that the scheme is still as vague as ever and I can hardly say, in the circumstances, that the question is being studied by the Board of Trade.' He went on to reiterate the Board's general policy in somewhat more sympathetic vein: insofar as the scheme tried to reduce trade barriers in Europe 'it has our sympathy', but he opposed a policy of more favourable customs treatment to countries within Europe than to countries outside. There was no reason to deprecate the exploration of the question providing our freedom of action in tariff policy was in no sense prejudiced.[9] The minutes reveal E.L.A. Robertson-Fullarton, Third Secretary in the Western section, fearing that Britain would not be welcome in a united states of Europe; Leeper opining that Briand's and Herriot's idea was indeed 'very vague' and had hardly any relation to Count Coudenhove-Kalergi's *Pan Europa*; Howard Smith noting again that Briand was committed to produce something for the next Assembly; and, not least, a dose of ministerial complacency from Dalton, Parliamentary Under-Secretary for Foreign Affairs:

> I am pretty sure that M. Briand hasn't got a scheme! It was necessary at the last Assembly, in view of the list of British initiatives, for the French to seem to be initiating something. Hence M. Briand's speech. M. Loucheur, on the other hand, probably has some approximation to a scheme in the back of his mind. But I shall be surprised if anything at all concrete emerges.[10]

In the spectrum of interpretation of Briand's federalist ideas, Dalton's notion of them as some sort of League virility symbol is one of the more arresting; it fitted neatly enough into the insular-reductionist pattern of response which found it hard to credit Briand's remarks with any real substance.

It was at this moment of confused and divided conjecture, and as if to upstage those who argued that there was little or nothing in these matters worth bothering about, that Tyrrell wrote dramatically to Vansittart:

> I have been informed in great confidence today [28 January] by Serruys that Loucheur is working on a Franco-German economic agreement to the exclusion of England. I am not quite clear what exactly this agreement, if it is at all immediate, can concern ... the Germans here seem to be hand in glove with the French at the moment, and the intimacy of their relations constantly surprises me and would probably very considerably startle people in London.

Tyrrell added a comment which suddenly revealed his own conception of

Europeanism:

> Serruys deplores what he states is the Loucheur policy, as he considers that the only way to bring about an economic recovery of Europe is by the cooperation of England, France and Germany; the policy I have always advocated, that of a real United States of Europe.[11]

Two days later, Tyrrell wrote again to suggest an Italian connection. He affirmed that

> my friend, who is in close contact with the German Embassy here, confirms the view that the French Government is now working very hard for a better understanding with Germany and that the vigorous pressure which is undoubtedly being increasingly exercised in that direction is due partly to the desire to cut out Italy with the Germans before it is too late.[12]

In a flurry of letters the Office sought to probe Tyrrell's warnings. His forebodings were passed on to Snowden, the Chancellor of the Exchequer, and Graham, the British Ambassador in Rome, whilst Rumbold, the ambassador in Berlin, was asked by Sargent what he thought of the spectre of Franco-German cooperation as raised by Tyrrell, and of rumours of intrigues between French and German nationalists – especially the so-called Rechberg plan. The conclusion of Sargent's letter to Rumbold illustrates the issues that were now believed to be associated with the federal idea and the Foreign Office's view of them:

> We are inclined to go a long way to discount the political aspects of these stories as vain imaginings of cranks and fanatics, but, even so, they tend to show the way politicians in these countries are still obsessed with the alliance idea which the League and the Kellogg Pact are supposed to have killed for good and all. Against this we have the more or less French official advocacy of the United States of Europe and of economic Franco-German cooperation, which it would be unwise to dismiss too summarily, even though we may not think that there is any danger of their being developed to an extent where they might threaten British interests.[13]

Vansittart's reply to Tyrrell himself sharpened the issues at stake and placed them in a more fundamental and historical context. Reflecting on Tyrrell's alarm at Serruys' account of Loucheur's policy, he commented:

Serruys' remarks remind us of Seydoux's article in *The Times* two years ago when he pressed us in the same way for British cooperation. The question then and now seems to be whether this desire for British cooperation is due to a genuine wish to save us from further isolation, economic or political, or rather whether its real object is to strengthen France against the economic pressure which Germany will be able to exercise over her to an ever-increasing degree if the two remain *tête-à-tête*.[14]

Tyrrell was also asked for his views on any connections between Franco-German nationalist intrigues and Loucheur's alleged activities.[15]

Tyrrell quickly returned to the fray with a letter on 11 February, having seen Serruys again and asked him why, periodically, this bogey of Franco-German economic cooperation was held over British heads.[16] Serruys argued that the British policy − as great traders and free trade theorists − of European cooperation by means of the lowering of tariffs was not the only one. There was also the French cartel or rationalisation theory based on the better organisation of production. What created the most deplorable impression, Serruys continued, was the way the British sought to impose their view on the French, when in fact what was required was a free and friendly dialogue via Geneva. But it was so difficult to talk with British officials: many of them did not seem able to understand the continental theory or talk the continental language. Serruys quoted Chapman in this connection.

This doctrinaire attitude had already exhausted the patience of influential people in both France and Germany. These people, headed by Loucheur, had got hold of Briand, who was also being pushed in the same direction by Léger. Serruys said that Loucheur and Léger, and under their influence, Briand, were definitely out for the federalisation of Europe on the economic basis of the organisation of production, rationalisation, etc., and that as Britain's attitude seemed to them so hopeless they were ready with Germany to organise Europe without her. Their ideas were still nebulous and they did not realise the dangers, but they thought they could organise Europe behind some kind of tariff barrier which would be erected to Britain's disadvantage and still more to that of the United States. Tyrrell added that the German embassy in Paris had told him that there was no difficulty between them and the French on the economic side of the organisation of Europe; it was on the political side that the difficulty lay. Serruys concluded that, whether the Loucheur or the opposite school of opinion finally obtained, the victory really depended on the attitude the British now took up. If Britain made the right noises 'we may keep this movement on [the] right lines and one from which we shall not suffer'. On the other hand, if the British continued with what the French considered hostile attitudes, 'I do think there is a possibility that an attempt will be made to proceed without us'. Vansittart duly communicated the contents of Tyrrell's letter to the President of the Board of Trade, though not without a note of scepticism:

> You will see that it all boils down to the suggestion that we have alienated the French and are driving them into an economic organisation of Europe with Germany from which we shall be excluded, and that if we are to avoid this we must meet the French half way in their views.[18]

Meanwhile Rumbold had written at length, summarising the chances of significant Franco-German economic cooperation at Britain's expense as negligible, defining Rechberg's influence as unimportant, and providing details of Franco-German industrial agreements and financial relations.[18] Rumbold's scepticism from Berlin as to the prospects of Franco-German cooperation at Britain's expense was clearly at odds with some of the possibilities Tyrrell had mooted from Paris. Sargent's and Vansittart's minutes reveal them agreeing with the implication of Rumbold's letter that there was little reciprocal feeling in Germany for either Franco-German economic or political cooperation, that is, for the French scheme for a united states of Europe. The crucial reasons were first, the centrality of the question of eastern frontiers — 'the Polish criterion' — and second, the wish to include Great Britain in any scheme of European cooperation. Nevertheless, Sargent argued, 'the future orientation of German foreign policy, now that the old problems are out of the way, is of the utmost importance on account of the repercussions it may have on Europe generally and for this reason we cannot watch it too closely in its initial phases'. Thus Sargent pondered the question of the way Germany might seek to re-open the Polish question, and thought that, if she approached it aggressively, she might abandon her current indifference to Italy, and join forces with her: 'It is evidently such a development which the Quai d'Orsay fears at the present time and which, I think, largely explains the efforts which are being made to attach Germany economically to France, with the collaboration of Great Britain if possible, but without it if such collaboration is going to delay or complicate matters unduly.'[19]

These minutes also mention the idea of a single memorandum nicknamed 'Old Adam' into which were being fed the synopses of the various issues under discussion which bore on French federalist plans, partly as a basis for making a response if at any time Briand were to come forward with concrete proposals later in the year. It is clear from the discussions that had taken place in January and February that French Europeanism was being placed in a far wider framework of reference than in 1929, as possible cause and effect of the emergence of a new era in European relations generally. The 'Old Adam' memorandum emerged in fact as an extended analysis of these more general themes, its preparation being masterminded by Vansittart. It was completed by the end of April and is discussed in detail at the end of this essay. Meanwhile the letter which Sargent wrote later in February to Sir R. Graham, the British Ambassador in Rome, stated that at least politically 'it is true that we have reached a turning point in European affairs ... and a new orientation is to be expected', and asked how Italy might fit in to the sort of scenario suggested by Tyrrell but questioned by Rumbold – especially with regard to the potentialities of Franco-Italian and German-Italian relations.[20]

* * *

In the midst of this reconnaissance came Tyrrell's awaited despatch on the Europe 'which France is organising', a key document in the pre-memorandum attempts to decode the problem.[21] Tyrrell placed current French federalist thinking firmly in the main traditions of French foreign policy. In its political aspect it was an extension, on the one hand, of the principle of ensuring French security by a policy of equilibrium, not conquest; a policy whereby France sought to preserve her supremacy by enmeshing her rivals in a moderate and peaceful diplomacy of treaty and alliance with non-rival states: thus 'by working for the general peace, France works for herself and assures her supremacy'. On the other hand, and more particularly, Tyrrell depicted French federalism as an extension of the policy of maintaining the predominance in Europe she had regained in the postwar settlement, not merely through the traditional means of treaties and alliances, but especially through the agency of the League of Nations. Central to this were the attempts made from 1918 onwards to vest the League with greater powers; to put the postwar settlement beyond doubt it was necessary to endow the League with powers of compulsory arbitration and the machinery for enforcing it. Thus, Tyrrell argued, the ultimate political organisation of Europe contemplated by France was not that formed by the network of alliances, mutual assistance and arbitration treaties concluded by her over the previous decade; it was a general system of compulsory arbitration and mutual guarantee such as was defined by the Geneva Protocol of 1924.

For Tyrrell, Herriot's words summed up French federalist aspirations: 'When France tries to federate the European countries, she is acting in the spirit in which she drafted the Protocol and in accordance with her traditional policy.' The question had surfaced in recent months because of 'the liquidation of the war', a phrase much in use to describe the latest stages in the amelioration of relations between allied and ex-enemy countries, especially France and Germany, which in turn reflected the apparent disappearance of many of the issues over which the First World War had been fought: for 'France realises that without German cooperation the political federation of Europe is impossible'. France would do all she could to get this cooperation, for she feared how German policy might otherwise develop, especially with regard to Italy. But, Tyrrell continued, the great obstacle to France was that the settlement she wished to maintain had in large part been effected at Germany's expense. Whilst France had in Europe a settlement she sought to preserve, would Germany, even in a federalised Europe, be content to renounce for ever modification of the *status quo*?

Tyrrell placed distinctly less emphasis on the economic aspect of the question. He said that the evidence of French international economic policy since the war indicated that the idea of the economic federalisation of Europe was not new: what was novel was the notion that discussion of even the economic side of European organisation should be transferred to diplomatic contact between governments. This would emerge at the tariff truce conference about to commence, as would France's doubts about the policy of general tariff reductions. Here there were disagreements with Britain, which one school in France wished to resolve through full and free discussion at Geneva. However, there was the other school, influenced particularly by Loucheur, and said to enjoy certain German support, which looked to the economic organisation of Europe through industrial agreements, based above all on Franco-German economic alliance, and proceeding in certain circumstances independently of Britain's attitude. Tyrrell thought that the economic side of French plans for European organisation was much vaguer than the political side, although progress on the latter side could produce a rapid resolution of economic difficulties. Anyway, there was no need to assume, as the Foreign Office had done when writing to Paris, that the two sides of the French scheme were being treated as interdependent. Their treatment had so far been kept distinct and would probably remain so. Tyrrell affirmed that the French would basically welcome British cooperation politically as well as economically, but doubted whether it would be forthcoming. If not, there would be a hardening of opinion to the effect that nothing can be done with the British. However, 'by a wise diplomacy we may keep this movement on lines from which we may benefit and need not suffer'. He concluded by underlining two profound forces for change in Europe. The first was the liquidation of the war, which might greatly and quickly change the character of Franco-German relations; the second was the growing recognition in France that without some closer political and economic organisation of Europe the future was too uncertain and dangerous.

This despatch, like its predecessors, provoked a plethora of comment, much of which was critical, some of which was divided. Leeper took the view that 'those [Frenchmen] who do realise that politically and strategically France is strong, see that economically her future is uncertain', and added that Tyrrell's view that the political and economic plans of France were likely to be kept distinct was hard to accept. He argued that it was the economic side of foreign policy that interested France most, and above all Franco-German cooperation. But he worried that, although both France and Germany wished for British cooperation, Britain might indeed not be able to offer it — and 'sheer necessity will bring them (however reluctantly) economically (and therefore in the long run, politically) together'. And he doubted whether the 'wise diplomacy' of Tyrrell's hopes, although enabling Britain to delay or modify the formation of an exclusive pan-Europe, would enable the British to remain 'in and out' of such a Europe – and to go in meant a definite economic break with the Dominions. Leeper added that Rumbold's evidence that the Germans were not at present rushing into France's arms disposed of some of his fears – but there remained the danger, supposing the British refused to cooperate fully in European reorganisation, of a Franco-German economic bloc leading to an economic united states of Europe arising sooner or later. Howard Smith minuted in the same spirit. To his mind the economic side was far more important and much more difficult for someone who was not an expert. Tyrrell's despatch really posed the whole question of future British commercial policy – and this was clearly beyond the sphere of any Foreign Office department. He thought that there might be a real danger in a policy of complaisance and that the question ought to be properly considered by the experts. On the other hand, Mounsey, the Assistant Under Secretary, doubted whether there was anything sufficiently concrete 'for even our experts to be able to formulate any...definite views as to the effects which such an economic policy would have on our own commercial fortunes'. Dalton was more sanguine: he found French political aims, as set out by Tyrrell, clear, and added sympathetically that 'in the next stage, that of completing compulsory arbitration, and adding to the Optional Clause of General Act, I hope and believe that H.M.G. can play an important part'. He found the economic aims cloudy and still adhered to the view that neither Briand nor any other French statesman had really worked out a scheme.[22]

Tyrrell's despatch was read most attentively, but his diagnosis of French federalism had not convinced his colleagues any more than his warnings of Franco-German entente. Above all it was not agreed whether the underlying motive of the Europe which France was organising was economic or political, or both.

* * *

What was becoming clearer was that whatever kind of Europe France wished to construct would not get far from the drawing board, inasmuch as it depended on significantly closer Franco-German political cooperation – or so Foreign Office officials came to believe as their reconnaissance reached its climax in late February and March.

On 28 February Rumbold wrote soothingly to confirm his view that Germany would for the next few years concentrate on her political and economic position at home in the first place, and that although she might take up the disarmament question with great vigour in the immediate future, the Polish question, for all its importance in the long term, was not an actual issue for the moment.[23] As Sargent minuted, and Vansittart agreed: 'this shows clearly ... that there is little danger of Germany embarking on a policy of foreign adventures. To that extent, therefore, Italy's hopes are as illusory as are French fears.'[24] A letter from Brussels, also on 28 February, in which Lord Granville reported that M. Hymans, the Belgian Foreign Minister, indicated that he neither believed that the French were definitely hostile to a tariff truce, nor that there was anything special going on in the way of a Franco-German rapprochement, provoked contrasting responses. Whereas Knatchbull-Hugessen, Counsellor at the Brussels embassy, thought Hymans was a little optimistic, Sargent minuted that it confirmed Rumbold's view that 'the Paris Embassy is perhaps inclined to exaggerate the extent and success of French attempts to bring about Franco-German cooperation, either economic or political'.[25]

Further evidence that the Paris and Berlin embassies were not seeing eye to eye was provided in a letter from Tyrrell to Sargent on 10 March, in which he rather tetchily took Rumbold to task for misinterpreting him:

> I certainly do not take Rechberg seriously and I have never indicated the possibility of <u>concrete</u> results in the matter of Franco-German cooperation in the immediate future. What seems to me undeniable, and what my despatches and letters have aimed at emphasizing, is the fact that, now that the liquidation of the war is practically complete, there are no longer the same reasons for difficult Franco-German relations as there have been during the last ten years.[26]

He accepted that the great difficulty was still the eastern frontier question and 'the key to the whole future of Franco-German relations lies in Berlin'. Sargent's minute reveals that the main episode in this investigation was now over: 'I don't think there is any point in sending this letter to Sir H. Rumbold. Continuance of this discussion is not likely to reveal any new truths which we have overlooked.'[27]

The Italian angle remained, and a long despatch from Graham on 14 March put three main points. First it argued that indeed the war had now, practically speaking, been ended: 'New orientations are developing, there are plans for still another new Europe'. Second, the fact that Italy did seem to be regarded as an essential factor in the Europe which France was organising vitiated the scheme, if this policy really aimed at creating a federalised Europe before improving relations with Italy. Third, Italy, fearful of the French hegemony since 1919, was certainly casting about for alternative support — but it was not yet clear in which direction. Sargent minuted that although Graham's despatch did 'not contradict any of the conclusions we have reached ... [it] will be extremely useful when we come to revise the draft memo'. Vansittart agreed: and again we have evidence of a general review of European relations emerging as an aspect of the consideration of French federalist thinking.[28]

Rumbold's scepticism about Germany's responses to French federalist ideas was set out afresh in his major despatch of 14 March. He argued strongly that most Germans would have found these ideas either too vague or else flatly hostile to the Europe of which Germany dreamt, because based on the European settlement of 1918 achieved at Germany's expense. In particular, he suggested that French official opinion was deceived, or deceived itself, as to the true nature of Franco-German relations if it assumed that the great problems that had discoloured those relations had disappeared — as if the Germans accepted, resignedly, their new eastern frontiers, which, Rumbold emphasized, they emphatically did not. Germany also suspected that federalisation might be directed against extra-European powers: and though she was more sympathetic to the economic aspects of federation, her basic attitude to the political aspect was one of hostility.[29] Rumbold followed this up with an assessment of German-Italian relations in which he confirmed the impression that neither Germany nor Italy had as yet taken any steps towards political understanding, and were not likely to do so for some time. However, Sargent minuted that Rumbold had shifted from his one-time view that Germany was not in the least interested in France's attempts to develop

Franco-German relations on the economic front. The fact that, in certain circumstances, France had something tangible to offer Germany was to be noted in the 'Old Adam' memorandum.[30]

Finally it is also clear from the minutes that, whereas an 'Old Adam' document reviewing the general European situation had been completed, no memorandum dealing specifically with French federalist proposals was yet considered worth producing. The materials for it were to hand and the basic line was that the whole federalist scheme was still so nebulous that Briand himself did not know what it meant. It was agreed to await the communication which Briand had promised before proceeding further.[31]

In answer to a request from the Chilean minister, in mid-February, for an expression of British views, Howard Smith summarised the Foreign Office position, or rather lack of it, as follows:

> I replied that we were still very much in the dark as to what M. Briand's intentions were ... The idea was not new and the Minister would find full information regarding it in the works of Count Coudenhove-Kalergi. It was not clear whether Monsieur Briand envisaged merely some kind of commercial union, or whether political considerations were also involved, but if his idea was that the states of Europe should join together in some kind of commercial union with preferential treatment between the members, I thought that the proposal would not be acceptable to His Majesty's Government, because it would cut across their commercial policy of most-favoured-nation treatment, which they had established all over the world.[32]

The hesitancy and scepticism of these remarks do not convey any real interest in or sympathy for their subject. And, in a written answer to a parliamentary question in March, Henderson confirmed that he was unaware that any further developments had taken place or that any specific policy had been tabled by France.[33]

Thus the prospect held out that Briand himself might wish to discuss his plans when he met Henderson in Paris early in May was treated almost as a threat. Howard Smith wrote that it was impossible to advise the Secretary of State, such was the absence of information about Briand's proposals, and all he could suggest was that Henderson should stall by saying that the British were waiting for his questionnaire before considering their attitude. Indeed 'in the present state of ignorance ... it would appear to be safer not to embark upon any discussion of the question if it can be avoided', Howard Smith advised.[34] European union had become unspeakable as well as unfathomable. In the event, Briand told Henderson that his questionnaire would shortly be published, and that the scheme had been drawn up in such a way as to keep it within the framework of the League of Nations and with due regard for the sovereign rights of individual states. Henderson promised to read the document with the greatest interest and he expressed the hope that there would be nothing in the scheme which would give it even the semblance of being directed against the U.S.A. Briand assured him there was nothing of the kind. Leeper, however, minuted that it was hard to see how any scheme of European federal union could fail to be directed in some way against American economic penetration.[35]

The narrative of this period can be concluded on a prophetic note. On 13 May Philip Noel-Baker summarised a conversation with the Finnish Foreign Minister, Procopé, who had asked for British views on French plans for a united states of Europe, and emphasized how opposed he was to anything that could be regarded as anti-American or anti-Russian, or that excluded Great Britain. Cecil minuted that he thought these views sound enough: and Leeper, with an eye to the immediate future, wrote: 'Everyone is anxious to have our views, but we want theirs.'[36]

* * *

This was hardly surprising. In one sense, officials had little to show for their labours since January: Europeanism as an aspect of French policy remained tantalisingly obscure. Tyrrell's formal assessment of federalist aspirations as central to French policy confirmed the realists' conviction that here was something that could not be dismissed lightly. Yet his emphasis on the dependence of French Europeanist hopes on Franco-German cooperation, abetted by his informal and alarmist warnings about how far and fast this cooperation was developing, backfired. Although a new flexibility in the relations between the states of Europe was generally admitted, the possibility of some kind of Franco-German political alliance foundered on the rock of

German unwillingness to accept any reorganisation of Europe that would embalm present, that is Versailles-based, territorial arrangements – or so British officials believed. Rumbold's role here was decisive; the sceptical line was sustained by the clear preference for his views over Tyrrell's in a conflict of ambassadorial advice. The upshot for most officials was that French federalist talk could be neither dismissed nor taken too seriously – a compromise verdict that partially vindicated sceptics and realists alike.

Official diagnosis of the specific content of federalist policy remained in animated suspense. Tyrrell's analysis of the political and economic dimensions provoked, as we have seen, mixed reactions. Most comment found it hard to follow his argument that the political and economic aspects were quite distinct, and that the political side was more central, and more developed, than the economic. Whilst one minister, Dalton, struck a sympathetic note about extending compulsory arbitration, officials remained silent about a revival of the Protocol idea; and Dalton's playing down of the economic side was matched by the real concern felt by officials at the possibility that Franco-German economic cooperation might lead where Britain could not follow. There was, therefore, no consensus as to what French federalist thinking involved, politically or economically; or indeed as to whether French conceptions of a united Europe were primarily political or economic. The desirability of a wise diplomacy to reconcile whatever the French might propose to British interests was undoubted; whether such a diplomacy was possible had to wait until it became clear what there was to be wise about.

Yet officials had not laboured wholly in vain. While the details of French federalist thinking remained obscure, its context had been clarified much more thoroughly than is usually appreciated. The link perceived between 'the Europe which France is organising' and Franco-German rapprochement had led officials to probe the implications of French federalism for French policy as a whole and for European inter-state relations generally. The survey of these wider horizons proved fruitful: much more sense was made of the international scene, and, in particular, of Britain's relations with Europe, than of French federalism *per se*. Further, these insights were embodied in a single document, Vansittart's 'Old Adam' memorandum of 1 May 1930, which provides the best summary to date of the framework within which officials diagnosed French Europeanism.[37] This framework, in turn, furnished the partly explicit, partly implicit, guidelines for the official assessment of Briand's proposals for European federal union when they were presented later in May. It is true that this was only the work of one individual, that it dealt with a single problem, and that it rejoiced in many idiosyncratic touches; but Vansittart was, after all, Permanent Under Secretary. One aspect – the dualism of forces for and against international peace and order – was a peg on which was hung a most wide-ranging review. As we have seen, this was based on a 'careful verification', involving the relevant Foreign Office departments, and 'particularly Mr. Sargent', together with the British ambassadors in Paris, Rome and Berlin.

The memorandum was shot through with a sense of the emergence, by 1930, of a new epoch in international affairs consequent upon the liquidation of the war. At the heart of this change was the 'recovery of Europe', and the object of the memorandum was to consider the implications of this recovery for the prospects of peace. These prospects were defined in terms of a duality: on the one hand, of the 'Old Adam', the aggressive, nationalist instincts of prewar origin that manifested themselves still, as they had before, in policies of armaments, alliances and balance of power; and, on the other, of the new postwar order of conciliation, arbitration and disarmament enshrined in the League Covenant and Kellogg Pact. What preoccupied Vansittart was the balance between these forces of darkness and light, and above all, which way the balance would be tilted by the policies of states as they responded to the opportunities opening up in the new era.

What is intriguing in the gospel according to Vansittart is not only the fatefulness he attributed to European states, and especially, to the problematic unfolding of the policies of Germany, Italy and France; there is also the unnerving enthusiasm for the role of Great Britain as angel of peace, harbinger of the new order and 'the most, indeed the only, international mind among our contemporaries'. Thus the memorandum elevated Europe, and British policy towards Europe, to the fulcrum of hopes for international peace, and the lack of any endorsement of Europeanism was all the more decisive. The complete indifference of official minds to the principle of a united Europe as an aspect of a preferred international society was abundantly, if negatively, confirmed.

There were, nevertheless, references to Europeanism. It was considered with some care and attention, but exclusively as an element in French policy. This, in turn, was discussed alongside a range of the policies of other European states, and the U.S.A. French policy was characterised as being dominated by the demand for security: France's 'sole concern' was the maintenance of the *status quo* and the preservation of the peace settlement. The methods France deployed to achieve these ends were various, and included the new principles and procedures of arbitration, conciliation, disarmament and the League of Nations – all of which were seen not as ends in themselves, but as means of sustaining French security.

Germany represented France's greatest problem: the memorandum cited French treaties with Poland and the Little Entente as evidence of a use of 'prewar architecture' in coping with this. But Franco-German relations showed much improvement; they were now 'normalised', and the memorandum probed the question of just how far Franco-German rapprochement might go. Although there was plenty of economic common ground, Vansittart reiterated the conclusion reached in the correspondence with Rumbold, and on which so much hinged: 'we may say ... that, notwithstanding the French efforts, Franco-German cooperation, economic or political, is not likely in the near future to develop in such a way as to acquire any great political importance.' Nevertheless, in launching Franco-German cooperation, France was also preparing a basis for the federalisation of Europe. The assertion of this linkage was followed by a familiar refrain: that French federalism 'is at present entirely nebulous, and M. Briand himself probably does not know what precise form he intends it to take'. The failure of official detective work, Vansittart implied, resulted not from the inadequacy of detection but from the lack of a body; the cupboard was – as yet – bare. The question remained, therefore, whether any French scheme would be primarily economic, organising Europe through industrial agreements and cartels, or, alternatively, through a German-style customs union; or, again, purely political, comprising a system of compulsory arbitration, general and mutual guarantees, general disarmament and peace-keeping machinery – which, the memorandum argued, would be a more sophisticated approach to the quest for security via the route of a revival of the 1924 Geneva Protocol.

Vansittart defined France's present anxieties as focusing on German aims and potential predominance, Italian hostility and the possibility of a German-Italian rapprochement. The lines of current French policy were defined in order as follows: the strengthening of the Kellogg-Briand Pact and of insurance against Italy, cooperation with Germany politically and economically, and the federalisation of Europe. Franco-German cooperation was rated, therefore, as more important than federalism, though not as the most important factor. The memorandum argued that if these policies did not yield results in security terms, France would turn, as her main means of defence, to her traditional alliance system with Poland and the Little Entente, and to building up her alliance with Yugoslavia to contain Italy. Vansittart urged that British policy should encourage France to opt for the policies involving the new machinery of disarmament and cooperation, and to take a 'broader and more liberal' view of this machinery.

In its conclusion, the memorandum returned again to the theme of Franco-German cooperation, only to repeat that it was something 'people talk of and don't see'. It was reaffirmed comfortingly that Britain was *not* going to be stranded: 'the [Franco-German] movement contains busy-bodies who must not be taken too seriously, especially when they try to make our flesh creep by urging that, unless we hurry up and get on the wagon, we shall be left out of Europe and rejected by the United States.' But the British had to be careful and keep watch, lest France's organisation of Europe 'showed signs of materialising without us ... could we stand aside, or must we admit our connexion with Europe and claim our place in a new European system? If so, what of the Dominions and the Empire?' Thus, despite the confidence that Franco-German cooperation would not get far, and that federalism was as yet too nebulous to be taken seriously, Vansittart was enough of a realist to recognise the possibility of the latter and pose relevant questions. He combined indifference to federalism in theory with a considerable respect for federalism in practice, precisely because it *was* French:

> All we can say of this important trend of thought is that any French scheme of federalisation will certainly be intended first and foremost, to guarantee French security, and will be suspect in the eyes of Italy as being tantamount to the establishment of French hegemony.

It was clear, therefore, that French federalism would probably not pose a great problem for Britain, but it could not be ignored; this conclusion transcended the tension between realists and sceptics by absorbing them both. As a policy it was rated fourth out of a possible six options open to France. The imprecision of its content meant that while it was clearly not a part of any 'prewar architecture', it was not easy to locate within the postwar patterns of international cooperation. Nevertheless Vansittart argued that as Britain and France differed on the means rather than the ends of policy 'Her [France's] schemes may be open to serious criticism; it is our business to turn them to better account'.

Thus, the 'Old Adam' memorandum did much to clarify the framework of French policy, European politics and the chances of a peaceful international order; yet its dominant theme was paradoxical. Europe was perceived as still very much the primary arena of international relations and the source of the most potent threats to peace; yet Europeanism was not considered other than as an aspect of French policy to be carefully monitored. In this context it was found on the one hand to be nebulous in content, suspect in motive, middling among the priorities of French policy, and unlikely to come to much; and on the other it was, or could be, important, it needed watching, and it might emerge as the sort of French policy whose principle could be amended or directed in the general international interest. It was this last possibility that hinted at a basis on which Britain might respond with other than scepticism or hostility to a French Europeanist initiative. This was emphatically not because of any sympathy with federalism *per se*, but as an extension of her concern – lauded in the memorandum as the essence of Britain's European policy – to lead the European states along the paths of international righteousness; along, that is, the postwar paths of cooperation and conciliation embodied above all in the League of Nations. Whether French federalism was in fact a suitable case for treatment was as yet unclear: it all depended on the presentation of Briand's proposals in concrete form.

Notes

1. This paper is a much enlarged treatment of an aspect of Ralph White, 'The British response to the Briand plan', in Andrea Bosco (ed.), *The Federal Idea: the History of Federation from Enlightenment to 1945* (London, 1991) pp.237-60. For a discussion of the Briand project itself, see Cornelia Navari, 'The origins of the Briand plan', in ibid., pp.211-36. For another view of the British response, see R.W.D. Boyce 'Britain's First No to Europe: Britain and the Briand Plan, 1929-1930', *European Studies Review* 10 (1980) pp.17-45.
2. PRO, FO 371/14069, W12163/153/17, Tyrrell to Henderson 29 December 1929; minute by Howard Smith 1 Jan. 1930.
3. Ibid., minute by Sargent 2 Jan. 1930.
4. Ibid., Howard Smith to Chapman 7 Jan. 1930.
5. PRO, FO 371/14365, C230/230/18, Tyrrell to Henderson 8 Jan. 1930 (W.N. Medlicott et al., *Documents on British Foreign Policy 1919-1939, Series 1A* (7 vols, London, 1966-1975) [hereafter *DBFP1A*], vol.7, no.183).
6. Ibid., minute by Carr 9 Jan. 1930.
7. Ibid., minutes by Howard Smith 9 Jan. 1930, and Vansittart 10 Jan. 1930.
8. Ibid., FO 371/14980, W451/451/98, Henderson to Tyrell 18 Jan. 1930 (*DBFP1A*, vol.7, no.213).
9. Ibid., FO 371/14980, W961/451/98, Chapman to Howard Smith 27 Jan. 1930.
10. Ibid., minutes by Robertson-Fullarton and Leeper 29 Jan. 1930, and by Dalton 3 Feb. 1930.
11. Ibid., FO 371/14365, C1002/230/18, Tyrrell to Vansittart 28 Jan. 1930 (*DBFP1A*, vol.7, no.231).
12. Ibid., FO 371/14365, C1032/230/18, Tyrrell to Vansittart 30 Jan. 1930 (*DBFP1A*, vol.7, no.233).
13. Ibid., FO 371/14365, C1002/230/18, Sargent to Rumbold 4 Feb. 1930 (*DBFP1A*, vol.7, no.237). The Rechberg Plan, according to secret sources referred to in Sargent's letter, was the plan of a faction within Hugenburg's Nationalist movement which favoured a military and economic understanding with France.
14. Ibid., Vansittart to Tyrrell 3 Feb. 1930. M. Seydoux was Deputy Director of Political and Commercial Affairs in the French Ministry of Foreign Affairs at the time; his article appeared on 15 March 1928 and official reaction is to be found in *DBFP1A*, vol.4, nos.167, 172.
15. PRO, FO 371/14365, C1002/230/18, Sargent to Tyrrell 6 Feb. 1930.
16. Ibid., Tyrrell to Vansittart 11 Feb. 1930 (*DBFP1A*, vol.7, no.243).

17. Ibid., FO 371/14365, C1234/230/18, Vansittart to W. Graham 14 Feb. 1930.
18. Ibid., Rumbold to Sargent 13 Feb. 1930 (*DBFP1A*, vol.7, no.246).
19. Ibid., FO 371/14365, C1358/230/18, minutes by Sargent 18 Feb. 1930, and Vansittart 23 Feb. 1930.
20. Ibid., Sargent to R. Graham 22 Feb. 1930 (*DBFP1A*, vol.7, no.251).
21. Ibid., FO 371/14365, C1570/230/18, Tyrrell to Henderson 17 Feb. 1930 (*DBFP1A*, vol.7, no.247).
22. Ibid., FO 371/14365, C1570/230/18, minutes by Leeper 24 Feb. 1930, by Howard Smith and Mounsey 25 Feb. 1930, and by Dalton 3 March 1930.
23. Ibid., FO 371/14365, C1753/230/18, Rumbold to Sargent 28 Feb. 1930 (*DBFP1A*, vol.7, no.262).
24. Ibid., minutes by Sargent and Vansittart 4 March 1930.
25. Ibid., FO 371/14365, C1840/230/18, Granville to Hugessen 28 Feb. 1930; minutes by Hugessen 7 March 1930 and Sargent 8 March 1930. The letter from Granville to Hugessen is found in *DBFP1A*, vol.7, no.263.
26. PRO, FO 371/14365, C1963/230/18, Tyrrell to Sargent 10 March 1930.
27. Ibid., minute by Sargent 12 March 1930.
28. Ibid., FO 371/14365, C2355/230/18R, Graham to Henderson 14 March 1930; minutes by Sargent and Vansittart 19 March 1930. Graham's despatch is found in *DBFP1A*, vol.7, no.281.
29. PRO, FO 371/14365, C2645/230/18, Rumbold to Henderson 14 March 1930: (*DBFP1A*, vol.7, no.280).
30. Ibid., Rumbold to Henderson 3 April 1930; PRO, FO 371/14365, C2694/230/18, minute by Sargent 9 April 1930.
31. Ibid., FO 371/14365: C2841/230/18, Tyrrell to Henderson 11 April 1930; minutes by Carr 15 April 1930, by Sargent and Vansittart 16 April 1930, and by Howard Smith 1 May 1930.
32. Ibid., FO 371/14980: W1882/451/98, 19 Feb. 1930.
33. House of Commons Debates, 5th Series, vol.236, cols 2154-5, 20 March 1930; discussion of reply PRO, FO 371/14980, W2936/451/98.
34. Ibid., FO 371/14980, W5193/451/98, Memorandum by Howard Smith 6 May 1930.
35. Ibid., FO 371/14980, W4922/451/98, Record of a conversation between Henderson and Briand 9 May 1930; minute by Leeper 15 May 1930. The conversation is found in E.L. Woodward, R. Butler et al., *Documents on British Foreign Policy 1919-1939, Second Series* (21 vols, London, 1946-1984), vol.1, no.185.
36. PRO, FO 371/14980, W5709/451/98, Record of a conversation between Procopé and Noel-Baker 14 May 1930; minutes by Leeper 23 May 1930, and

Cecil 29 May 1930.
37. Memorandum by Vansittart 1 May 1930: 'An aspect of international relations in 1930', Appendix to *DBFP1A*, vol.7.

Great Britain and the French Resistance

M.R.D. Foot

'What French resistance?' was Albert Speer's first reply when an interrogator asked him what impact French resistance had had on German war production; that is, at his ministerial level it had been imperceptible. It did not seem quite the same on the ground, but it is important to remember that, at the start, there was very little of it indeed. From London, all that could be observed in the late summer of 1940 was the gloomy presence there of Charles the Tall, with whom only five thousand Frenchmen had elected to stay and fight, out of the tens of thousands brought back from Norway and from Dunkirk to British ports. Most had had enough of battle, and wanted to go home.

A very few people, in the innermost circles of Whitehall, knew of Major (eventually General) Gustave Bertrand, who was holed up at a château near Uzès in Provence, with the survivors of the Polish team of very bright mathematicians who had been reading German 'Enigma' machine-ciphered messages, on and off – more on than off – since 1932.[1] Bertrand was in W/T [wireless/telegraphy] touch with Bletchley Park, in another cipher; the Gestapo's writ did not as yet run far in Pétain's two-fifths of France governed from Vichy, so for the time being they were safe. They worked in deadly secrecy, but were no longer critically important, because Bletchley's own serious inroads into Enigma were now starting to show results. Anything Uzès could provide was by now marginal, not central.

The very first agent the British sent into France was presumably Philip Schneidau, recruited – so J.C.Masterman once claimed in conversation with me – by Masterman (then an MI5 agent) in the changing-room after an international hockey match. Schneidau carried out an in-and-out mission, in by parachute and out by Lysander, in the early autumn of 1940. He returned, with difficulty, on the night of 19/20 October.[2] What news, if any, he brought back with him remains unrevealed. I once met a man at the BBC who claimed he had been parachuted into France the night before the armistice (that is, on 21/22 June); he did not explain how or when he returned, and this is not a story history needs to accept.

A few of the best and the bravest of the French were already busy thinking about how they might resist. But the bulk of the population took the realist view that defeat was defeat, and that one had better accommodate oneself as best one could with Authority, personified after all in the Marshal who had saved the nation in 1917. Any stay-behind parties that SIS [Secret Intelligence Service] might have thought of had been organized from The Hague, where a junior's indiscretion had left undestroyed a list of all the relevant addresses. This was in the Gestapo's hands by mid-May 1940 to supplement what the Germans had picked up already from the captives at Venlo.[3]

An example of early French resistance activity at its best – but also at its most ingenuous – can be found in Martin Blumenson's *The Vilde Affair,* which is devoted to the splendid group at the Musée de l'Homme, who knew what they should do, and most of them died for doing it.[4] They did not know any of the elementary rules of the clandestine life, and were early prey to policemen and to double agents. Moreover they had no contact with London: such intelligence as they could collect was not therefore usable in the anti-Nazi war effort.

Contact with London did exist, in an unexpected way, for Marshal Pétain. I have not found it easy to forgive the Foreign Office for never having dropped the least hint to me, when I was working on my *SOE in France* thirty years ago, of what this channel had been.[5] Pétain had had a short spell as French ambassador in Madrid – a token gesture by the Third Republic to show that the Popular Front's anti-Franco feelings were now muted. While there, he had met at a cocktail party a second secretary at the British embassy, a speaker of fluent French with whom he got on well and exchanged Christmas cards in 1939. In 1940 the second secretary dared to send him another Christmas card. He got an amiable reply, and was used by the Foreign Office as a private channel of approach to the old man. The 1983 publication of letters revealing the existence of this channel has been described as like a new window opened on to the inner history of the war's diplomacy.[6] The channel certainly deserves more attention than most historians have so far given it.

SOE [Special Operations Executive] of course was quite another kettle of fish: not a diplomatic organization at all, and a cause of incessant headaches to the Foreign Office. Its first mission into France was to have taken place in November 1940; but the agent, having had a good look at moonlit Brittany through the hole in the floor of his Whitley's fuselage, announced that he was not going to jump. Like any other refusing parachutist, he was sent back whence he had come the moment the plane landed; and as he made a perfectly respectable career elsewhere later in the war, I see no point in making a bogus sensation by revealing his identity. In March 1941, with operation 'Savannah', SOE began serious business; raising, right from the start, awkwardnesses for the diplomats. De Gaulle had not yet been recognised as head of a government – indeed never was recognised as such, by the Americans or by the British who here followed dutifully in their footsteps, until October 1944, by which time he had returned to France and been acclaimed there.[7] The Russians were cannier, and recognised him in September 1941.[8]

SOE's 'F', or independent French, section was set on its feet largely by the efforts of the three de Vomécourt brothers, Lorrainer barons educated in England and as strongly pro-British as they were anti-Nazi – not a perfectly normal attitude for a French citizen in the early 1940s. They spent a vast amount of effort and plenty of their own money in organizing the earliest groups who were prepared to do some sabotage. They too got entangled with double agents. Pierre de Vomécourt's wireless operator was arrested; he found another through the agency of the only too celebrated Mathilde Carré, 'La Chatte'.[9] He thought she was working for SIS, through some Polish friends, but in brute fact she was working with Sergeant Bleicher of the Abwehr.[10] De Vomécourt was lucky to be allowed to spend the second half of the war in Colditz instead of being shot out of hand.

A constant theme in the British attitude to French resistance was the interplay of intelligence services versus what the French called *service action*, sabotage and subversion. Of course, there were rivalries between SOE and SIS. For these there was an excellent professional reason: if SOE's agents did their job, they would be found, by creating mayhem, to attract police attention to their area, which was exactly what SIS agents wanted to avoid. Equally, within SOE, there were rivalries between F Section, the independent French, and RF Section, the Gaullist section. And within indigenous French resistance, there were plenty of rivalries too – not only between local chieftains, a Frenay or a Coulaudon who wanted to have his own way in his own province, but between those who looked to de Gaulle and those who looked to Stalin – the *Francs-Tireurs et Partisans*, the communist-animated resisters who followed Moscow's orders, and from 22 June 1941 joined in whole-heartedly against the Nazis. There were those moreover – not many, but some, and some who were influential – who looked to Roosevelt, and tried to negotiate with Allen Dulles of OSS [Office of Strategic Services] when the latter reached Switzerland, as he did just before the frontier closed in November 1942.

It was indispensable for those French who wanted to fight to get in touch with some outside power who would provide arms: for active resistance, arms are as indispensable as rain for a farmer. The trouble about doing so was the frightful insecurity (or so at any rate it seemed to the British and to the Russians) of almost every Frenchman and Frenchwoman. Everywhere, people *will talk*, which is how security and police services get their work done. This common failing of mankind seemed to be specially prevalent in Pétain's France. Ben Cowburn, now the oldest surviving F section *chef de réseau*, who went on his first mission at Pierre de Vomécourt's elbow in 1941 and parachuted in on his fourth in July 1944, once said that 'security in France was nil, and 95 per cent of the people arrested were caught simply because their friends had been incapable of keeping their mouths shut'.[11]

Ostensibly the largest, and undoubtedly one of the least secure, of F Section's circuits in France was 'Carte', the creation of André Girard the painter, who adopted 'Carte' as his own codename, and took no other security precautions of any kind. He attracted the attention in turn of Peter Churchill,[12] and also of Nicholas Bodington, F Section's second-in-command, supposed to be one of the informers planted in SOE by the unspeakable Colonel Dansey of SIS.[13] Bodington spoke so highly of 'Carte' when he returned to England that SOE approached the Chiefs of Staff for an increased air lift, in order to supply it. Although the circuit was entirely notional, this *grande illusion* did perform one strategically useful function: it got the Chiefs of Staff accustomed to the idea that, if they wanted help from the populations of occupied Europe, they were going to have to reduce the number of heavy aircraft they allotted to the bomber offensive so that they could drop supplies instead.[14]

The Gaullist French took up with enthusiasm and care the practical problems of supply-dropping, which are legion at the ground end – let alone the fearful complications of planning and security that attend anything of this sort at the sender's end.[15] Two half-nationwide bodies, the *Bureau d'Opérations Aériennes* [BOA] in the northern or fully occupied zone, and the *Service d'Atterrisages et Parachutages* [SAP] in the southern, provided wireless liaison with SOE's RF Section in Dorset Square, Marylebone, reception committees on the ground, and safe hiding-places for what came down. In addition they arranged for distribution to the agents who were going to do the actual work of sabotage or direct attack on the enemy. Without the BOA and the SAP, French resistance would have been powerless; without the RAF's special duties squadrons, the BOA and the SAP would have had no *raison d'être*. Close links today between the survivors of all three bodies were forged in furnaces of peril.

In parallel with RF Section's attempts to get the nation organized for a major upheaval whenever the Allied invasion took place, F Section's agents — who have had a great deal more publicity on this side of the Channel — were working to a narrower, but not less important, brief. Their task was to carry out specific acts of sabotage, to fulfil instructions from the Chiefs of Staff and hamper German communications as well as production. To do this surely, F Section's circuits needed to keep small: an awkward task, once the tide of the war had started to turn, and the brasher organizers found themselves surrounded by eager and enthusiastic French citizens, longing to blow something up. Francis Suttill, in charge of the 'Physician' F circuit that centred on Paris, was a Lincoln's Inn barrister who spoke good enough French to pass in Paris for a Belgian. 'Physician' snowballed — too many enthusiasts joined up with it, of whom in turn too many were unwary enough to be entrapped by double agents, some local, some imported from Holland. 'Physician' — usually referred to by Suttill's own codename, 'Prosper' — fell with a catastrophic thud in the summer of 1943, bringing several hundred French men and women down with it.

Suttill's friend Henri Déricourt sailed through the 'Prosper' catastrophe untouched: *bon déricourtiste* as always, working busily with both sides and collecting money, including £15,000 for three betrayed F Section agents, but not, I fancy, actually betraying Suttill, whom he liked. Suttill in fact betrayed himself, by falling into the habit of playing cards most evenings with his closest fellow-agents (all of whom fell with him) in the same café in Montmartre.

'Prosper' was by no means alone. Besides F and RF, and DF, the escape section, and EU/P, the section that dealt with the large Polish minority in France, and the 'Jedburgh' teams who did not arrive (in uniform) until Normandy D-day, there was another SOE section working into France from late 1942, which has not had all the attention from historians that it deserves. This was 'AMF', which operated out of Algiers into southern France. There are no AMF archives – the head of section burned them all, on being ordered to close down in September 1944.[16] But quite a lot is recoverable, if one knows where to look – RAF operational record books, the wastes of FO371, and the ever-helpful SOE Adviser in the Foreign and Commonwealth Office who can provide translations for codenames. In fact AMF seems to have sent more agents into France than either F or RF did. Most of them went to assist 'Dragoon', the Provençal landings that were so much helped by resistance.[17] Many of the agents sent by AMF were American, and belonged to the OSS. This came comparatively late to the field, but by 1944 was contesting as an equal or even a superior to SOE in the secret struggle against Hitler.[18] More of OSS's effort into France was made into the southern zone to support 'Dragoon' than into the northern zone to support 'Overlord', apart from the OSS participation in every 'Jedburgh' team. The bulk of the operational groups, OSS's rival to the British SAS, worked into such areas as the Vercors.

There, the French succumbed to the myth of the national redoubt – the area that was to be cleansed of all trace of Nazi occupation, to welcome the allied armies by being already liberated when they arrived – that had such dire consequences in Poland, Slovakia and Serbia as well as in France. De Gaulle hoped for a national insurrection, to coincide with the allied landings (of the date of which he had to be kept uninformed). By contrast, Gubbins, who ran SOE, hoped rather for a serious effort in direct support of 'Overlord' and 'Dragoon', in particular for support for 'Neptune', the assault phase of 'Overlord', the Normandy landings of 5/6 June 1944.[19] Gubbins won. The 950 rail cuts carried out by agents and sub-agents using SOE's plastic explosive on the night of 'Neptune' between them paralysed the French railway system, thus forcing the German army's reinforcements on to the roads, where the RAF and the USAAF could disrupt them. A much less widely publicised, but still important, set of parallel operations put the long-range French trunk telephone system out of order, thus forcing the

Germans on to R/T [radio/telephony] and W/T – in turn providing even more raw material for deciphering and increasing the flow of intelligence. I must also mention one agent by codename at least – 'Alphonse', whose sabotage teams, one of them consisting of two sisters, the older of them just turned sixteen, crippled the tank transporters of the 2SS Panzer Division at Montauban and thus delayed its arrival in Normandy from D-day + 3 to D-day + 17: an ideal instance of the value of subversive tactics.

De Gaulle had had to be kept uninformed of the date of the Normandy landing for a simple, highly secret reason: the ciphers that he insisted on using were insecure. SOE's cipher officer was once able to break a Gaullist cipher instantly, in the presence of several senior Gaullists.[20] The latter were duly impressed, and adopted the one-time pad for operations – but continued to use their own, worthless ciphers for politics. There was a steady stream of political traffic between the Gaullists in Algiers and their rear link in London, through which many of their communications with agents in the field had to run; this was a standing danger. Yet de Gaulle won, as well as Gubbins. Those who rallied to his name were active all over central and southern France, and played a much more vigorous part in repelling the German garrisons scattered round the country than city-centred French historians have yet brought themselves to admit. Roderick Kedward's new book provides an indispensable source on this crucial point.[21]

While 'Dragoon' was being planned, a copy of the outline plan was passed to de Gaulle in Algiers; and he showed it to General Zeller, who had just come out of southern France. Zeller did not like it, and, when asked by de Gaulle what he thought of it, had to reply – this was how one expressed disagreement with the great man – '*Mon Général, je ne serais pas complètement d'accord.*' What upset Zeller was that the phase map showed Grenoble as liberated on D-day + 90, by an advance up the Rhône and the Isère, by which time, he reckoned, all the many resisters in the Alpine foothills would be dead. Could the advancing Americans not try to use the Route Napoléon, through Digne and Gap, to get to Grenoble faster from a flank ? Zeller was sent across to Naples to see the American General Patch who was to command 'Dragoon'; and as Arthur Funk's *Hidden Ally* explains so well, his plan worked. Grenoble fell on D-day + 7, and most of Zeller's friends survived.

At the same time as the many sabotage and subversive teams of SOE were beavering away in France, there were a lot of intelligence *réseaux* busy as well. These have not yet received much attention from historians writing in English. But they provided both cover and insurance for the ultra secret work being done at Bletchley Park by the Government Code and Cypher School, for which Sir Harry Hinsley and others have provided a magisterial official history.[22] All the members of one of the largest and most efficient of these networks of spies took the names of birds or animals for their codenames, and so were nicknamed 'Noah's Ark' by the Gestapo; their organizer, Marie-Madeleine Fourcade, took the nickname as the title for her post-war account of their triumphs and disasters.[23] It is a mark of the gulf that still divides French historians from accurate knowledge of how the British secret services worked that de Gaulle's latest and best biographer affirms that Fourcade was working with SOE – in which nobody, I think, had heard of her before France was liberated.[24]

Colonel Rémy's circuits were comparably important, and some of them have been described in English.[25] I can myself testify to the godsend provided, indirectly with Rémy's help, by a fortunate theft when the Germans began to build their West Wall of Channel coast fortifications. The Organisation Todt had a headquarters near Caen from which the building operations were planned. Staff moved in before the building had been properly done up; a house-painter called René Duchez removed a copy of the specifications for reinforcing the concrete in the various sizes of pillbox and casemate, and it was smuggled out. Gunners planning coastal bombardments could have asked for nothing more specific.[26]

Besides SOE with its plethora of networks, and SIS with the same, quite another British secret service was working into France during the war – MI9, which looked after escapers and evaders, and came rather remotely under the wing of SIS. Escape, like espionage, is one of those subjects which attract the media's sensation-mongers only too readily. Many splendid stories, some of them true, have emerged from this side of the French resistance. Time allows reference now to only one development on this front – the emergence in the summer of 1944 of a new spectator sport, parachute-watching.

To take part, you needed a bicycle with a basket, and some

old clothes – a pair of shoes, a jacket or a sweater, a pair of trousers. When a squadron of passing Allied aircraft got involved in an air battle, and parachutes started to fall, you bicycled towards them; and hoped you would arrive before either the French or the German police. If you did, you helped the airman out of his flying suit (which you buried, if you had time and had remembered to bring a spade; your wife kept the parachute) and put your old clothes on him; and hid him in the barn or the woodshed. In a few hours' time, someone would come from an escape organization to take him away. This was not quite as simple as it sounds; particularly if a double agent arrived to collect the airman – and you – instead of someone from an escape line. But MI9 had France so well sewn up that the odds on an airman shot down over France in July or August 1944 getting back to his squadron within a month were as low as evens.[27]

None of this could have been attempted without strong encouragement from the French, whose morale had swung a very long way since the summer of 1940, when the northern bourgeoisie had bolted and the peasantry had not cared who won or lost. After four years of the Nazis, hostility to them had become intense, fanned by broadcasts from abroad as well as their various excesses in France. The names of Churchill and de Gaulle had both become household words, and almost everybody outside the *milice* was by now on their side.

Notes

1. Bertrand swallowed the Poles' own cover story about how they started to break Enigma, as revealed in Wladyslaw Kozaczuk, *Enigma: how the German machine cipher was broken, and how it was read by the Allies in World War II* (London, 1984). See G. Bertrand, *Enigma: ou la plus grande énigme de la guerre 1939-1945* (Paris, 1973). Yet the present writer's copy bears a certificate, in Bertrand's hand, that anything in any other book that contradicts it is false!

2. H.B. Verity, *We Landed by Moonlight* (London, 1978) pp.35-8, 198.
3. On the Venlo incident, see Christopher Andrew, *Secret Service* (London, 1985) pp.434-9.
4. M. Blumenson, *The Vilde Affair* (Boston, 1977).
5. M.R.D. Foot, *SOE in France* (London, 1966; revised edn, 1968). H.M.S.O. sold the rights of this book to the University Presses of America, which then went bankrupt. But it is still in print, courtesy of Greenwood Books, though a long way from the original price of forty-five shillings.
6. David Eccles (ed.), *By Safe Hand: Letters of Sybil and David Eccles 1939-42* (London, 1983). The description was that of the historian, Ronald Lewin, not long before he died.
7. See A. Dansette, *Histoire de la Libération de Paris* (Paris, 1966; 1967 edn.) pp.410-2.
8. Brian Crozier, *De Gaulle* (2 vols, London, 1973) vol.1, pp.179-80, 194.
9. M-L. Carré, *I Was the Cat,* trans. Mervyn Savill (London, 1961) provides the case for her defence.
10. Hugo Bleicher, *Colonel Henri's Story*, ed. E. Borchers, trans. Ian Colvin (London, 1954), with all its faults, conveys some of the atmosphere of Paris under the occupation.
11. Foot, *SOE in France* p.121. Cowburn was speaking in December 1944.
12. Q.v. in *Dictionary of National Biography 1971-80* (Oxford, 1986) p.149.
13. Q.v. in *Dictionary of National Biography: Missing Persons* (Oxford, 1993) pp.171-2.
14. See P.M.H. Bell, *A Certain Eventuality: Britain and the Fall of France* (Farnborough, 1974) p.50.
15. Cf. M.R.D. Foot, *Resistance: European Resistance to Nazism 1940-1945* (2nd.edn, London, 1977) pp.122-6.
16. Foot, *SOE in France* p.450.
17. See Arthur L. Funk, *Hidden Ally* (New York, 1992).
18. See George C. Chalou (ed.), *The Secrets War* (Washington, 1992) pp.295-300.
19. See Peter Wilkinson and Joan Bright Astley, *Gubbins and SOE* (London, 1993).
20. Foot, *SOE in France* p.241; and private information.
21. H. R. Kedward, *In Search of the Maquis* (Oxford, 1993).
22. F.H. Hinsley et al., *British Intelligence in the Second World War* (3 vols, London, 1979-1988); see also F.H. Hinsley and A. Stripp, *Code Breakers: Inside Story of Bletchley Park* (Oxford, 1993).
23. M.-M. Fourcade, *L'Arche de Noé* (Paris, 1968). An abbreviated translation appeared as *Noah's Ark* (London, 1973).
24. Jean Lacouture, *De Gaulle,* trans. P. O'Brien and A. Sheridan (2 vols,

London,1990-1993) vol.1, p.371.
25. E.g., Gilbert Renault-Roulier ['Colonel Rémy'], *The Silent Company* (London, 1948) or *Courage and Fear* (London, 1950).
26. Richard Collier, *Ten Thousand Eyes* (London, 1958) pp.78-88.
27. M.R.D. Foot and J.M. Langley, *M19* (Boston, 1980) pp.216-7.

Eden, de Gaulle and the Free French: un bienfait inscrit dans la mémoire?

Christine Giuliani

Perhaps it would have been better if he could have forgotten things more.[1]

In a stimulating recent article Philip Bell, a self-confessed francophile, argued that Charles de Gaulle, leader of the Free French during World War Two and first President of the Fifth French Republic, failed to appreciate the debt which he owed to Great Britain for services rendered during the darkest days of recent French history after the fall of the country in June 1940.[2] De Gaulle's personal survival and the re-emergence of France as a major force in European and world politics owed much to Britain's wartime protection, even though relations at a personal level were never easy. The chequered interaction between de Gaulle and Winston Churchill has been well documented.[3] Two such powerful characters were almost bound to clash, and there developed 'a tangled situation of formidable personalities'.[4] If de Gaulle did fail in later years to repay his debt to Britain, memories of the insults, real and imagined, received at the hands of the British war leader were no doubt at the forefront of his largely psychological and emotional attitude. It is, however, at least arguable that the individual to whom de Gaulle and the whole Free French movement owed most was not Churchill but his Foreign Secretary, Anthony Eden. De Gaulle himself seemed to appreciate his debt. In his war memoirs he subsequently wrote that Eden 'showed an openness of mind and a sensitiveness that were European rather than insular, human rather than administrative'. Above all, 'Eden felt a special affection for France. From her he had derived a large part of his culture.'[5]

Eden succeeded Lord Halifax at the Foreign Office when the latter was appointed to the Washington embassy in December 1940. He remained in post at Churchill's side, recognised from 1942 as his designated successor, until the defeat of the Conservative party at the 1945 General Election. The post was, of course, the same one from which Eden had resigned in February 1938, exasperated by the interference of the then Prime Minister, Neville Chamberlain, in the affairs of his department. In many ways Eden experienced something of the same problem when serving under Churchill. There were those who believed that it was in effect the Prime Minister who ran British foreign policy during the war years. Oliver Harvey, a senior Foreign Office official of the time, noted soon after the start of the postwar Labour government that its foreign policy was 'much of what Anthony's policy would have been if he had ever been allowed to have one'.[6] Yet this was unfair to the Foreign Secretary. Eden was no cypher. It is true that there were areas of British diplomacy, most notably Anglo-American relations, which Churchill tended to reserve for himself. But in a number of other fields Eden's role was crucial. The development of policy towards de Gaulle and the Free French was perhaps the most important, and even this always had an American dimension. Eden indeed once described the triangular relationship between Britain, the United States and France as the 'principal [diplomatic] problem of the war'.[7]

It was not, however, Eden's style to leave his mark through confrontational opposition to the Prime Minister. His partnership with Churchill was always of a more complex nature than some critics appreciated. Certainly he had a surer grasp of many of the key diplomatic issues of the war than did his master. Rather like Alan Brooke in the field of strategy, it was often Eden's task in diplomacy to resist and eventually filter out the Prime Minister's wilder flights of fancy, leaving the occasional brainwave to see the light of day. It was a role which called for finesse and patience – qualities which Eden displayed in abundance, even though he was sometimes driven to the point of private rage and distraction by Churchill's more unreasonable whims. A private secretary recorded that Eden sent 41 separate minutes to the Prime Minister over a fifteen week period in 1944 on the single issue of General de Gaulle.[8] Working with Churchill was an exhausting experience. 'I am so weary I hardly care', Eden confided to his diary in 1944.[9] But the Foreign Secretary generally seemed to know when to give way to Churchill, when to stand his ground, and when to use his very considerable powers of persuasion and charm. 'More argument about France', he noted later the same year, 'the drip drip of water on a stone.'[10]

An episode in the spring of 1942 exemplifies Eden's technique. With de Gaulle wishing to visit Africa and the Near East, the Foreign Secretary intervened on his behalf. There was, he insisted to Churchill, no adequate reason for refusing the General facilities to visit 'his own territories'. Any attempt to do so would merely increase his suspicions of Britain which 'are seldom far below the surface'. 'In these circumstances', Eden concluded, 'I hope you will agree that for the sake of our future relations with him it would be best to let him go.'[11] Churchill, however, seemed immovable, his personal feelings submerging his reason: 'I cannot agree. There is nothing hostile to England this man may not do once he gets off the chain.'[12] Yet Eden skilfully transformed Churchill's intransigence into a suggestion that the British government might wish to consult de Gaulle on critical matters relating to the war and that it would therefore be inadvisable for him to leave London.[13] With the General mollified, Eden was in a better position to tackle the Prime Minister again:

> You will see that he is prepared to adjourn his visit for at least six weeks. He really was reasonable about it. ... But if I have been able to put his journey off for six weeks, I hope that you will help me and that some attempt will be made to consult him a little in regard to events present and future.[14]

Eden's was often a thankless task, but in the field of Anglo-French relations his conduct seems to have been wise and far-sighted.

That Eden should emerge as the leading champion of France inside the British government was by no means obvious in the early stages of the conflict. His reaction, as Secretary of State for War, to the fall of France in 1940 seems to have been that the country had experienced such great shame that she could never rise to prominence again, whatever the outcome of the war as a whole.[15] An early difficulty over General de Gaulle provoked the half-serious remark, 'I hate all Frenchmen'.[16] But Eden was first and foremost a Foreign Office man and he soon came to accept the line of his department that the re-creation of a strong France must be a primary British war aim. Particularly after 1942 the Foreign Office was actively considering the position of Britain in the postwar world. The future security of the United Kingdom would involve the drawing together of the nations of western Europe, especially in the expectation that the United States could not be relied upon to maintain a military presence on the continent at the end of hostilities. As part of a western European bloc, of which she would naturally be the leader, and maintaining her position at the head of the Commonwealth,

Britain could sustain her Great Power status into the years of peace. Within Europe itself one scenario pictured the dangers of a revived Germany; a second pictured a power vacuum in central and eastern Europe with no barrier to the westward expansion of the Soviet Union. In either case the role of a restored France would be critical. Thus France seemed likely to emerge as more central to Britain's postwar interests than even the United States, notwithstanding the latter's immediate importance in securing military victory. As Eden once put it, France was a 'geographical necessity'.[17] Despite his internationalist credentials, carefully nurtured during the 1930s, Eden was ready to adopt a balance of power approach to the future of Europe – something which was bound sooner or later to run up against the liberal idealism of the United States.

Furthermore, it rapidly became clear to the Foreign Office that the revival of France was synonymous with the person of General de Gaulle. It was an equation which the General himself often made – much to the irritation of those, including Churchill, who found his inflated egotism intolerable. At the fall of France de Gaulle was largely an unknown quantity in Britain. 'I can't tell you anything about de Gaulle', said Sir Alexander Cadogan, Permanent Under-Secretary at the Foreign Office, after his first meeting with the General, 'except that he's got a head like a pineapple and hips like a woman.'[18] Soon, however, it became difficult to ignore this self-appointed leader of the Free French movement. William Strang, who played a major role in drawing up Foreign Office policy in this area, later summed up de Gaulle's importance:

> The Foreign Office at once recognised the significance of de Gaulle. From the time of his establishment in London, through his turbulent sojourn in Algeria, down to the time when he entered a liberated Paris and duly became the head of a recognised Provisional Government, they fostered the Free French movement, accorded it progressive degrees of recognition, and bore with what patience and understanding they could the storms that he let loose upon them. This was, above all, Eden's policy.[19]

De Gaulle, of course, had a rather different view of France's future from that pondered inside the British Foreign Office. As he subsequently recorded:

> the war's end would leave us in force on the continent, while

America would be back in her hemisphere and England on her
island. Provided that we knew what we wanted, we would then
have the means to break out of the circle of resigned acceptance
and docile renunciation inside which our three partners intended
to imprison us.[20]

But such differences were for the future. For the time being there existed a
basic community of interest between Eden and de Gaulle.

In the pursuit of his policy Eden faced two enormous and inter-related
obstacles. The first was the American government. The United States
administration inevitably adopted a more sceptical attitude than did the British
Foreign Office towards French pretensions to great power status. There was
no doubt that France had been badly defeated. It was at least questionable
whether she intrinsically merited the postwar standing envisaged for her by
Eden and others. 'The British', Roosevelt noted in 1943, 'wanted to build up
France into a first class power, which would be on the British side.'[21] But
there were obvious reasons why the United States should not subscribe to
such an objective. Additionally, America was slow to admit that a postwar
France headed by General de Gaulle was the only viable option. Indeed,
there were good grounds for supposing that some form of the Vichy regime,
which had already accepted the supremacy of Nazi Germany, might more
easily fall under the postwar sway of the United States, allowing that country
economic concessions and military bases in its colonial empire, than would
a France headed by an independent-minded de Gaulle.

Personal chemistry was important here. Some American politicians were
more clear-sighted than others. As de Gaulle consolidated his position,
Secretary for War Henry Stimson concluded that the General had to be
recognised in the wider interests of Anglo-American relations. But on this
issue President Roosevelt and his Secretary of State, Cordell Hull, spoke with
a single voice. 'President's absurd and petty dislike of de Gaulle blinds him',
Eden confided to his diary in March 1944.[22] But if Roosevelt was difficult
on this question, Hull seemed beyond reason. 'He hates de Gaulle with such
fierce feeling', noted Stimson, 'that he rambles into almost incoherence
whenever we talk about him.'[23] There were issues of high policy where
Roosevelt treated the views of his Secretary of State with scant regard. The
latter's role in wartime diplomacy was never comparable to that enjoyed by

Eden. On this issue, however, where Hull and his master were essentially of one mind, his opinion could not be discounted. Eden could only come to the conclusion that the Secretary of State had 'an obsession against [the] Free French which nothing [could] cure'.[24]

The second obstacle standing in the way of Eden's smooth conduct of Foreign Office policy towards de Gaulle was the not inconsiderable person of the British Prime Minister. Churchill came to share Roosevelt's irritation at de Gaulle, annoyed by the General's exaggerated sense of his own dignity and importance. De Gaulle left an account of a meeting with Churchill at 10 Downing Street in September 1942 at which the Prime Minister dropped all pretence of diplomatic nicety: 'You claim to be France! You are not France! I do not recognise you as France!'[25] Yet for a year after the fall of France it was far from clear that the Prime Minister would emerge as an impediment to Eden's policy. Early in 1941, at a time when the Foreign Office was still reluctant to shift its support from the Vichy regime to de Gaulle and the Free French, Churchill seemed ready to take a different line. Deputising for Eden at the Foreign Office, he sent a revealing minute to Cadogan: 'An end should be put to the cold-shouldering of General de Gaulle and the Free French movement, who are the only people who have done anything for us, and to whom we have made very solemn engagements.'[26] But Churchill's repeated criticisms of the Foreign Office went largely unheeded.[27] At much the same time Eden was speaking of France in the sort of unsympathetic terms for which he was later to criticise the Prime Minister: 'The French want us to win the war to rescue them, but they still want to receive the produce of their colonies, even including wine, though they pay toll 80% to the enemy, who will then be better placed to fight us.'[28]

It was, however, above all else the American dimension which came to divide Prime Minister and Foreign Secretary on this issue. By the end of 1941 at the latest, Eden had concluded that the resistance movement in France and also the majority of French opinion overall were overwhelmingly behind General de Gaulle. This consideration was fundamental to his postwar vision. Though at times a self-styled 'Atlantic animal',[29] and a man who had been brought to the verge of resignation from Neville Chamberlain's government in January 1938 because of the then Prime Minister's cold-shouldering of Roosevelt's half-baked peace initiative, Eden genuinely believed that Britain's relationship with France would have a higher postwar priority than her association with the United States. This was something which Churchill could never accept. The courting of America, and of President Roosevelt in particular, had been central to his strategy since the outbreak of hostilities in September 1939. Thus, as American opposition to de Gaulle became clear, Churchill was ever more ready to follow Roosevelt's lead on this matter so as to maintain good Anglo-American relations. Eden, on the other hand, believed that Churchill was too willing to adopt a subservient attitude towards the United States which was not in Britain's best long-term interests. This difference in perspective would cause Eden considerable problems during the course of the war. He later described the situation in the sort of low-key terms which characterised most of his memoir writing:

> Apart from any sentiment he might harbour towards General de Gaulle himself, Mr. Churchill was naturally reluctant to be at odds with the President if he could avoid it. Nevertheless he was usually patient with the arguments which I pushed remorselessly in dozens of messages and conversations.[30]

In fact, Prime Minister and Foreign Secretary probably clashed more bitterly over de Gaulle and the Free French movement than any other wartime issue and, by his own later admission, Eden excluded from *The Reckoning* many of the more revealing entries from his diary which would have offered a clearer picture of his relationship with Churchill.[31] Those around them, however, were left in no doubt of the strength of feeling on either side. 'I hope A[nthony] and P.M. will fight it out between them on the telephone', recorded a weary Cadogan at the beginning of 1943.[32]

* * *

De Gaulle's first major confrontation with Britain occurred in June 1941 over the joint British and Free French military operation against Syria. After the surrender of the Vichyite regime an armistice was signed which hardly mentioned the Free French. De Gaulle was inclined to interpret this as an attempt by Britain to transfer French colonial territories to British jurisdiction and reacted by threatening to remove his Middle East troops from British

command. The episode led finally to concessions by the British but it also did
lasting damage to de Gaulle's relations with Churchill. Eden was clearly
anxious to repair the rupture. He proposed a meeting between the two prima
donnas:

> It may be we shall find that de Gaulle is crazy; if so, he will have
> to be dealt with accordingly. If, however, he shows indications of
> repentance, I hope that you will not underestimate your power to
> complete the cure. He has a real and deep respect for you.[33]

In reply, Churchill showed that he could stand on his dignity as readily as de
Gaulle himself:

> No notice will be taken of General de Gaulle's arrival, and it will
> be left to him to make any overtures. Should he desire an
> interview, he will be asked for explanations of his unfriendly
> conduct and absurd statements. If and when these explanations are
> received, it will be possible to judge whether an interview between
> him and me is likely to serve any useful purpose.[34]

A pattern had been set which would characterise the following three years.

As the United States proceeded to play an ever more active role in the war
and, in December 1941, to become a belligerent, continuing American ties
with Pétain's Vichy regime were bound to create difficulties for the Allies'
relations with the Free French. America's policy was to retain contacts with
Vichy in the hope of bringing Pétain round to an anti-German position. Most
observers in Britain were always sceptical of this objective and conscious of
the difficulty of selling it to a British public which held Pétain and his regime
in low esteem after the capitulation of 1940. On this specific issue differences
between Churchill and Eden were largely of emphasis, though they did little
to discourage the Prime Minister's view that his Foreign Secretary was
unnecessarily soft towards de Gaulle and the Free French. Churchill stressed
that it was most important for the United States to maintain their relations
with Vichy – 'there is always time to break but it is more difficult to renew
contracts'.[35] Eden agreed in principle 'provided the Allied war effort will
be helped thereby'. Of this, however, he remained doubtful. The policy of
Vichy, he asserted, was to maintain France's quasi-neutrality and to derive
every possible advantage from continued contact with the United States 'by
blackmail over the French fleet and bases'.[36] The danger, moreover, always

existed that any military advantage would be far out-weighed by damage at the long-term political level.

Eden presented his growing doubts on this question to the cabinet on 1 June 1942. Here he stressed that resistance in occupied France was now synonymous with Gaullism and that the General was accepted as the leader and symbol of Free France. Allied dealings with Vichyite alternatives could have disastrous consequences in the future.[37] Churchill remained unconvinced and the debate between the two men rumbled on through an increasingly acrimonious exchange of minutes. The Prime Minister tried to bring the dispute to a close by insisting on his own strongly francophile instincts, while presenting Eden's position as unacceptably narrow and rigid:

> For thirty-five years I have been a friend of France and have always kept as closely in touch as possible with the French people. I therefore have a certain instinct about them on which I rely. It is very easy to make the kind of case you have set down out of all the shameful things the Vichy Government have said. But this does not make sufficient allowance for the unnatural conditions prevailing in a defeated country with a Government living on the sufferance of the enemy... The position is so anomalous and monstrous that very clear-cut views, such as you are developing, do not altogether cover it.[38]

This time Eden felt that he must stick to his guns. He returned to the attack the following month. De Gaulle's failings were, he admitted, well-known. His sudden actions could at times be dangerous. He was intensely suspicious and felt deeply, like all true Frenchmen, the humiliation of his country. And yet –

> we must give him credit for having kept the flag of France flying by our side since June 1940. We have been largely responsible for building him up in France, and it is clearly impossible for us to drop him now ... His disappearance would have a bad effect on the forces of resistance in France where, as numerous recent reports show, his value is growing as the recognised symbol of resistance to Germany.[39]

Eden's patience with de Gaulle was not inexhaustible and renewed problems over Syria, where the General talked of pushing the British out of

French territory if they failed to meet his terms and of insisting that the Allied command in the Levant should be in French hands, left the British Foreign Secretary less disposed than usual to tolerance. Eden recognised that the forthcoming Allied invasion of North Africa – Operation Torch – might well transform 'the whole perspective of the French problem. We may hope as a result of that for a wider Fighting French organisation and one which will show more statesmanship than the present quarrelsome clan.'[40] He urged Churchill to use the opportunity of a meeting with de Gaulle to deliver a homily on his general behaviour. 'We are tired', the Foreign Secretary confessed, 'of the series of crises into which, on the slightest pretext, he throws Anglo-Free French relations.'[41]

Such thinking may help to explain the somewhat equivocal role which Eden played in relation to the notorious Darlan affair, when the American command in North Africa patched up an opportunistic agreement with a former minister of the Vichy regime. As Philip Bell has pointed out, Eden had been present at the crucial discussion at which contact with Darlan had been aired and had not tried to block the idea. But the Foreign Secretary had certainly not changed horses. He had been uneasy throughout about the exclusion of Free French forces from Operation Torch and was soon anxious once more to assuage de Gaulle's feelings. After trying unsuccessfully to gain agreement to bring the General into the planning of the administration of liberated areas of France, he helped secure a commitment for the transfer of Madagascar to the General's authority once the North African landings took place.[42]

Over the Darlan deal itself, Eden's misgivings rapidly increased. In mid-November Lord Cranborne, his closest political colleague, warned of the possible dangers:

> You are, I'm afraid, going to have great difficulties in getting rid of Darlan … It is a deplorable business, as it will give the worst impression both in France and the other occupied countries of what will happen after the war. Our protestations against war criminals will look very hollow – I feel with you that you must, if possible, get some telegrams off to Washington, stipulating at any rate that we shall not recognise him in any way as representing a civil government. There are limits beyond which

cynicism should not go.[43]

On the same day a 'deeply disturbed' Eden, 'moved to the point of tears', succeeded in convincing de Gaulle that Churchill's readiness to follow this particular American policy was distasteful to him personally.[44] The sincerity of the Foreign Secretary's emotions is impossible to gauge, but the experience of being heckled on this issue in the Commons can only have increased his desire to distance himself from everything to do with Darlan. 'He manages', recorded Harold Nicolson, 'to imply that he does not agree with the action of Eisenhower in giving Darlan authority, but that he begs the House to be discreet.'[45]

Behind the scenes Eden raised the matter with Churchill, leaving no doubt as to his own opinion:

> Our appeal to the French people, whose resistance has been steadily stiffening, is now stultified. We shall not be able to speak to them with a clear voice until the Vichy element has been eliminated from the French administration in North Africa... I do not underrate the military reasons for General Eisenhower's deal with Darlan: but I feel strongly that if we do not eliminate Darlan <u>as soon as the military situation permits</u> we shall be committing a political error which may have grave consequences not only for our good name in Europe but for the resistance of the oppressed people for whose liberation we are fighting.[46]

Churchill persuaded Eden to leave things as they were for the time being. But the situation was inherently dangerous. As Cranborne pointed out, without a *modus vivendi* between the British and American governments on this question, the ultimate possibility was that each country would end up committed to its own French client and then 'we shall have a serious row'.[47] The Americans, Eden concluded, were becoming 'increasingly tiresome over Darlan, and almost everything else'.[48] Only the intervention of an assassin on Christmas Eve removed both Darlan and the difficulty which his position created.

* * *

Darlan's death did little to deter American enthusiasm to rid the Allies of de

Gaulle. The United States' championship of General Giraud in the course of 1943 was bound to strain Anglo-American relations while causing further difficulties between the British Prime Minister and his Foreign Secretary. De Gaulle's reluctance even to meet Giraud drove Churchill to one of what were becoming his typical outbursts:

> The man must be mad to jeopardise the whole future of the relations of his movement with the United States. ... If in his phantasy of egotism he rejects the chance now offered I shall feel that his removal from the headship of the Free French Movement is essential to the further support of this movement by H.M.G ... For his own sake you [Eden] ought to knock him about pretty hard![49]

Eden, however, preferred arguments more firmly based on notions of British self-interest:

> I have never in my experience had dealings with anyone with whom it was more difficult to do business. ... But there are two things to be said in his favour. The first is that he is unlikely now or hereafter to collaborate with the Germans ... The second point I would make is that de Gaulle, whatever his faults, and they are serious, is a more vital and dynamic personality than anyone else who has come to the front.[50]

With Churchill warning Eden on no account to allow Britain's relations with the United States to be spoiled through patronage of a man 'who is also our bitter foe and whose accession to power in France would be a British disaster of the first magnitude', Eden clearly faced a difficult task when he visited Washington in March.[51] His close colleague, Oliver Harvey, summed up his dilemma:

> A.E. is between the hammer and the anvil. For British interests we are all convinced that we should work with de G ... The P.M. is passionately persuaded that de G is our enemy, that he will work against us now and even after that he means to bedevil Anglo-American relations.[52]

In the event Eden stood by his convictions, refusing to give ground to Hull or Roosevelt.[53] It was striking that when the American president told a press conference that he and the British Foreign Secretary were 95% in agreement, the outstanding 5% related largely to France.[54] It had now become clear to Eden that the United States did not want to see the establishment of any single French authority, even if that authority was not yet recognised as a government. His subsequent report to the cabinet indicated his own mounting irritation with the American leadership.[55]

When Churchill followed his Foreign Secretary to Washington in May, he proved more susceptible than Eden to American pressure. Roosevelt mounted a consistent series of complaints about de Gaulle's intolerable attitude and 'Messianic complex'. Under such a barrage, and ever mindful of the priority of the American alliance, Churchill asked his colleagues back in London to consider whether the moment had not come for de Gaulle to be eliminated as a political force. Eden and the Labour leader, Clement Attlee, took the lead in resisting the Prime Minister. With signs that de Gaulle and Giraud might at last be coming together, the two men warned that the existing members of the French National Committee and even the Free French fighting forces were unlikely to function if de Gaulle were removed from the scene.[56] In response Churchill insisted that it must be for the Foreign Office to argue its own case:

> I have no intention of marring my relations with the President by arguing in the sense of your various telegrams. The only channel for such discussions must be the Foreign Office and the State Department. I have given you my warning of the dangers to Anglo-American unity inherent in your championship of de Gaulle.[57]

In the last resort, however, Churchill agreed to await the outcome of forthcoming talks between the two French generals and urged the Americans not to push the matter to the point of a quarrel with Britain.

Eden had won a battle, but not yet the war. De Gaulle had survived, somewhat unwittingly, his most serious crisis since the fall of France. Had Churchill and Roosevelt prevailed in the early summer of 1943, the consequences for Anglo-French relations would have been incalculable. Over the following weeks Eden could not afford to relax. As one historian has put it,

> these French affairs provoked numerous crises, heated controversies and late night wrangles between the Prime Minister

and his Foreign Secretary during June and the better part of July.
Every time Churchill grunted, scowled, growled and snarled, but
Anthony Eden always emerged victorious in the end.[58]
A 'fierce but friendly' argument between Prime Minister and Foreign
Secretary on the night of 12/13 July lasted until 2 a.m. A memorandum
submitted by Eden at lunchtime saw the atmosphere worsen. Churchill even
'thought we might be coming to a break'.[59] But, as was often the case, it
was the Prime Minister who had to move his ground. 'I'm beginning to know
the form now', recorded Harvey. 'Frightful rows, nervous exhaustion on
both sides, the next day a rather contrite P.M. seeking to make up, like a
schoolboy who knows he's been naughty.'[60] A paper drawn up by Churchill
for the War Cabinet in which he had described de Gaulle as showing 'many
of the symptoms of a budding Führer' was not circulated.[61] Within a week
the Prime Minister was remarking that he seemed to have 'swallowed
[Eden's] thesis whole'. In the Foreign Secretary's view it amounted to
'asking Americans to face up to the realities of our situation'.[62] At all
events, by the end of the month the Prime Minister's line had markedly
softened: 'It is de Gaulle's duty to regain the confidence of the two rescuing
Powers. If he will do his part, I will do mine.'[63]

* * *

From mid-1943 there were new battles to be fought as Eden, conscious that
attention would soon have to be given to the problems of the peace, set about
securing formal recognition for de Gaulle's French Committee of National
Liberation. Restrictions of space preclude more than a cursory survey of what
followed. Eden put the case for the recognition of the French Committee at
the Quebec Conference in August. Limited progress was made with
Roosevelt agreeing to recognise the FCNL as administering only those
territories which it actually held. Once the conference was over, the President
expressed the view that he would have been able to make much more
progress with Churchill on this matter but for Eden's presence.[64] At the first
of the great wartime gatherings of the Big Three at Teheran in November,
Eden had to protect de Gaulle from fresh assaults, this time emanating from
the Soviet Union. He resisted the suggestion of Foreign Minister Molotov

that the entire French nation should be stigmatised as collaborators and argued for the acceptance, when the time came, of liberated France as a friendly country rather than a former enemy.[65] The year's end gave Eden the opportunity to remind Churchill of the vital strategic role which France would play in the postwar balance of power on the continent: 'Though the Bear's manners are steadily improving, I have still no ambition to share the cage alone with him.'[66]

As the allied invasion of Europe approached, it became increasingly urgent to settle the outstanding issues relating to France and particularly the question of recognition. 'We must get French business settled and Winston won't take decisions on this', Eden noted in April 1944. 'He sympathises too much with F.D.R.'s anti-de Gaulle complex.'[67] By the beginning of June the Foreign Secretary sensed that he was making progress:

> Spent best part of an hour there with W. Much talk about French with usual arguments bandied to and fro and W. slowly coming nearer our point of view and emphasising concessions he had made.[68]

But even on D-Day itself the two men were still quarrelling over the same issue:

> I was accused of trying to break up the government, of stirring up the press on the issue. He said that nothing would induce him to give way, that de Gaulle must go. F.D.R. and he would fight the world. I didn't lose my temper and I think that I gave as good as I got. Anyway I didn't budge an inch.[69]

Making little progress with the Prime Minister, Eden turned his attention to de Gaulle, inducing the French leader to open discussions with the British. 'A.E. tired but triumphant this morning', noted a private secretary, 'having brought de Gaulle along considerably at dinner last night and then carried Colonel Warden [Churchill], though it took him till 3 a.m.'[70]

In the end it was the course of events in France which finally resolved the question of recognition. In July the FCNL was recognised by the United States as the 'temporary *de facto* authority' in France. Thereafter so spontaneously did the liberated French rally to de Gaulle that Roosevelt was left with little alternative but to accord formal recognition as the Provisional Government of France on 23 October 1944. Eden himself remained a doughty champion of French – and, as he saw it, British – interests until the end of the war. He found it difficult to 'contemplate a future in which France will not be a factor of considerable importance'.

> She must be interested in almost every European question. If we do not have her cooperation, she will be able – not at once perhaps – to make difficult the application of any solution which does not suit her.[71]

By the time of Yalta Eden had the backing of Churchill and it was largely thanks to British pressure that France emerged from the conference with the trappings of great power status restored to her. The two men were coming to agree that, as Eden put it, 'General de Gaulle is not a permanency, but France, we hope, will be and we want to build her up'.[72]

It had been a long struggle, but one in which Eden had been both clear-sighted and consistent. On the question of de Gaulle Churchill had too often allowed his emotions to get the better of his reason. Cadogan saw the reality of the situation:

> P.M. ended with a tirade against de G. 'He has been battening on us and is capable of turning round and fighting with the Axis against us.' That is just untrue. Tiresome he may be, but sound on essentials.[73]

But Eden was the vital safeguard as a result of which Churchill's Gaullophobia never quite overcame his essential francophilia. The Prime Minister's dislike of de Gaulle had been exacerbated by his sometimes unquestioning subservience to the American president. The great difficulty, Eden once confided, was that Churchill was half-American and regarded Roosevelt with almost 'religious awe'.[74] Eden, on the other hand, recognised Roosevelt as an astute politician, but one who understandably placed American self-interest before everything else. The British Foreign Secretary was equally determined to give priority to British interests: 'I have little doubt myself that FDR does NOT want us to take the lead in Europe and equally no doubt that we should.'[75] For this reason he was prepared to indulge de Gaulle to an extent Churchill often found intolerable. De Gaulle, with little to back his pretensions, wanted Britain to treat France with a respect which successive British governments had found it difficult to feel for perhaps the last decade of the Third Republic, when France had at least been an independent nation. But Eden, often criticised for his reluctance to plan beyond the short-term, was in this instance prepared to take a longer view. For him, therefore, the Cross of Lorraine, though heavy to bear, was never totally insupportable. 'Do you know', Eden once asked the General, 'that you have caused us more difficulties than all our other European allies put together?' 'I don't doubt it', replied de Gaulle, 'France is a great power.'[76] Seeing the problem from their differing perspectives, the two men were at least agreed on this point.

* * *

There is a postcript to this story. Philip Bell has argued that de Gaulle, in his later career, showed scant gratitude for the support which he had received from Britain during the Second World War. Anthony Eden might well have seen matters in a different light. The postwar careers of de Gaulle and Eden scarcely overlapped. Illness had compelled Eden's resignation from the premiership, and from an active role in public life generally, in January 1957, more than a year before de Gaulle returned to power to inaugurate the Fifth Republic. In his years of retirement, however, Eden continued, naturally enough, to interest himself in the great affairs of state. The Suez Crisis of 1956 left him with a lasting feeling of resentment towards the United States. The priority given by his successor, Harold Macmillan, to the restoration of the severely damaged Special Relationship was bound to cause him considerable irritation. Less than a year into the new government Eden wrote contemptuously that Macmillan's policy was 'making us the 49th state'.[77] Inevitably, therefore, his views drew him closer again to General de Gaulle.

Eden usually managed to visit Paris at least once a year during his retirement. Lunch with the General and a private discussion *à deux* became part of his routine. On one such occasion de Gaulle took Eden into the garden of the presidential palace and expressed the hope that, after a period of recuperation, the former premier would soon be able to make a complete return to public life. Eden was flattered, but could only explain that his series of major operations since 1953 had left him incapable of again withstanding the pressures of high office.[78]

It is clear that these meetings between the two men usually produced a uniformity of outlook. Of a visit to the French President in the spring of 1961 Eden wrote:

I had a good talk with de Gaulle. ... Upon the world scene we find ourselves only too closely in agreement about its very sombre prospect. ... I have no doubt he feels some resentment, as we do, at the American outlook on colonial matters. His argument was that we understand that an evolution has taken place but we want to do it by our own methods and in our own time. ... I do not think that in broad matters the present French administration wish to be in any way stand-offish. On the contrary, I think that they would value closer relations but think that we are so much tied up with the Americans that these things are hardly realizable.[79]

At this particular meeting the issue of the European Economic Community did not come up for discussion. In the early 1960s, however, the question of Britain's possible membership of what was then usually called the Common Market was a matter of particular concern to Eden.

The issue of Britain and Europe was one on which he was remarkably consistent over a period of two decades. He was what, in the parlance of a later generation, would have been called a 'Eurosceptic'.[80] His most notable pronouncement on the subject remains the address which he delivered to Columbia University in January 1952 when accepting an honorary degree. Here Eden stressed the positive role which Britain had played in the postwar reconstruction of Europe. There could be no question of 'turning our backs' on the continent. But, as regards the idea that the United Kingdom might join a European federation, he was absolutely clear: 'This is something which we know, in our bones, we cannot do.'[81] In adopting such an attitude Eden always insisted that he was at one with Winston Churchill. But the latter's apparently pro-European rhetoric in the late 1940s encouraged others — especially those who did not read his speeches very closely — to believe that his own commitment to the European ideal had been undermined by Eden. A decade after his Columbia address the attitude of Eden, by then ennobled as the First Earl of Avon, had scarcely changed. It was one of the few issues which could persuade a man who was by then under doctor's orders severely to restrict his public appearances to re-enter the political arena. In a letter to a leading anti-Market Conservative M.P., Eden wrote:

> Apart from the Common Market negotiations we are, as I understand it, pledged to further talk about political union. What can this mean except Federation and I do not believe it right for this country to federate with France, Germany and Italy as the political outlook is today.[82]

There is some evidence that Eden worked behind the scenes to try to marshal the opposition within the Conservative party against Macmillan's decision to seek British membership of the Common Market.[83] His attitude was founded on the belief that Macmillan was not prepared to come clean about the ultimate political implications of a body which was presented to the British public as little more than a trading organisation. Like de Gaulle himself, Eden favoured a 'Europe des patries' rather than a federal super-state.[84] And he believed that Macmillan had been 'wrong to funk the federation issue'.[85] A difficulty, he told an audience of Young Conservatives in June 1961, was that the six existing member states of the Common Market had not as yet themselves determined what their final objective should be. But federation was possible under the Treaty of Rome and Britain must be told what would be expected of her in all respects before she could take a decision:

> What we must not do is to join any organisation without a full understanding of its implications and then find ourselves being swept further than we intended. Once the decision is taken, it will be too late to complain.[86]

When in July 1961 the Macmillan government first announced that it had decided to make a formal application for British membership, there seemed to be a range of obstacles in the Prime Minister's path, offering comfort to a doubter such as Eden. Even a year later a like-minded Labour M.P. reminded him that the Commonwealth issue was 'crucial'. 'Fortunately Gaitskell is good on this; and so are enough of your backbenchers, I think.'[87] One by one, however, the immediate obstacles and difficulties facing Macmillan were apparently overcome. In parliament there existed a group of up to fifty Conservative sceptics – though there were also Labour supporters of British membership. As, however, the crucial Commons vote in August 1961 had been merely to enable the British negotiating team to see whether satisfactory arrangements could be reached to meet Britain's existing obligations to the Commonwealth and E.F.T.A., the government had had no difficulty in securing a majority. Neither in 1961 nor in 1962 did the Conservative party conference offer much resistance to the leadership. The gathering of Commonwealth Prime Ministers in September 1962 revealed considerable misgivings about the British application, but in the last resort the delegates had to accept – since they would demand no less for themselves – that ultimately a decision about the future of Great Britain belonged only to the British government. By the autumn of 1962, therefore, it appeared that all immediate domestic obstacles had been cleared from Macmillan's path. On the assumption that the negotiations themselves could be brought to a satisfactory conclusion, there remained only the readiness of the existing members of the Common Market to accept Britain into their midst. In practice all depended on the attitude of General de Gaulle. As is well known, the French President exercised what was in effect a veto on British membership at his celebrated press conference on 14 January 1963.

There seems little doubt that Eden felt greatly relieved by de Gaulle's decision. In a somewhat perverse way the General had repaid his debt from twenty years before. The two men had met again in June 1962, when the question of Britain's application had certainly been on the agenda. It seems unlikely, however, that Eden – always the most discreet of politicians – did anything to undermine the negotiating position of the British government. He did, however, emphasise the official line that it was important to make arrangements to safeguard the wheat, meat and dairy trade of Australia and New Zealand, and stressed that if satisfactory terms could not be reached, 'we would have to go on as we were'.[88] A later meeting, after de Gaulle had exercised his veto, resulted in an interesting discussion between the two men:

> I told him I was puzzled by his policy because I'd always been taught that France wanted Britain in Europe so that she was not left alone with Germany. Now however she did not seem to want us. De Gaulle replied: 'But I am following Churchill's policy' and he picked up a volume of W[inston]'s speeches and read out the passage in the Zurich speech [of 1946] which visualised France and Germany together in Europe and ourselves with the British

Commonwealth and United States (and he hoped a friendly Russia) lending support from without. 'That is what I am doing' asserted de Gaulle firmly.[89]
It seems reasonable to suppose that Eden felt that justice had been done all round.[90]

Notes

1. Eden of de Gaulle: transcript of Eden interview with Kenneth Harris, 1975, Avon Papers [hereafter AP] 7/23/591. Extracts from the Avon Papers at the University of Birmingham Library are reproduced by kind permission of Lady Avon and the Avon Trustees.
2. P.M.H. Bell, 'La Grande Bretagne, de Gaulle et les Français Libres, 1940-1944: un bienfait oublié ?', *Espoir* 11 (1990).
3. See, in particular, François Kersaudy, *Churchill and De Gaulle* (London, 1981).
4. AP 7/23/591, transcript interview.
5. C. de Gaulle, *The Complete War Memoirs* (New York, 1984) pp.230-1.
6. Harvey to E. Evans 26 Aug. 1945, cited P. Hennessy, *Never Again: Britain 1945-51* (London, 1992) p.255.
7. AP 7/23/590, note by Eden 20 Oct. 1975.
8. P. Dixon, *Double Diploma: The Life of Sir Pierson Dixon, Don and Diplomat* (London, 1968) p.93.
9. AP 20/1/24, diary 24 March 1944.
10. AP 20/3/9, diary 12 Oct. 1944.
11. AP 20/9/115, Eden to Churchill 27 May 1942.
12. AP 20/9/115A, Churchill to Eden 30 May 1942.
13. Kersaudy, *Churchill and De Gaulle*, p. 187.
14. AP 20/9/506, Eden to Churchill 4 June 1942.
15. J. Colville, *The Fringes of Power: Downing Street Diaries*, (pbk edn, 2 vols, London, 1986-1987) vol.1, p.250.
16. Ibid., p.481.
17. Lord Moran, *Winston Churchill: the Struggle for Survival 1940-1965* (London, 1966) p.501.
18. D. Dilks (ed.), *The Diaries of Sir Alexander Cadogan* (London, 1971) p.302.
19. D. Dilks (ed.), *Retreat from Power: Studies in Britain's Foreign Policy of the Twentieth Century* (2 vols, London, 1981) vol.2, p.74.

20. De Gaulle, *Complete War Memoirs* pp.722-3.
21. G. Kolko, *The Politics of War* (pbk edn, New York, 1990) p.73.
22. AP 20/1/24, diary 4 March 1944.
23. Kolko, *Politics of War* p.83.
24. R. Dallek, *Franklin D. Roosevelt and American Foreign Policy 1932-1945* (Oxford, 1979) p.408.
25. De Gaulle, *Complete War Memoirs* p.341,
26. Dilks, *Cadogan Diaries* p.356.
27. Kersaudy, *Churchill and De Gaulle* p.131.
28. Minute by Eden 26 Jan. 1941, cited in R.T. Thomas, *Britain and Vichy: The Dilemma of Anglo-French Relations 1940-42* (London, 1979) p.56.
29. Lord [Robert] Boothby, *Recollections of a Rebel* (London, 1978) p.211.
30. Lord Avon [Anthony Eden], *The Reckoning* (London, 1965) p.447.
31. AP 33/3, Eden to R. Blake 15 Aug. 1963.
32. Dilks, *Cadogan Diaries* p.502.
33. AP 20/8/537, Eden to Churchill 31 Aug. 1941.
34. AP 20/8/675, Churchill to Eden 1 Sept. 1941.
35. AP 20/8/708, Churchill to Eden 30 Nov. 1941.
36. AP 20/9/13, Eden to Churchill 5 Feb. 1942.
37. PRO, CAB 66/25, WP (42) 233.
38. AP 20/9/359, Churchill to Eden 14 June 1942.
39. AP 20/9/515A, memorandum for Cabinet 8 July 1942.
40. AP 20/9/185, Eden to Churchill 22 Sept. 1942.
41. AP 20/9/543A, memorandum by Eden 22 Sept. 1942.
42. Thomas, *Britain and Vichy* p.141.
43. AP 20/39/30, Cranborne to Eden 16 Nov. 1942.
44. De Gaulle, *Complete War Memoirs* p.362.
45. N. Nicolson (ed.), *Harold Nicolson: Diaries and Letters 1939-1945* (London, 1967) p.263.
46. AP 20/9/286, Eden to Churchill 26 Nov. 1942.
47. AP 20/39/40, Cranborne to Eden 17 Dec. 1942.
48. AP 20/39/40A, Eden to Cranborne 21 Dec. 1942.
49. PRO, CAB 120/76, Churchill to Eden 18 Jan. 1943.
50. AP 20/10/41, Eden to Churchill 2 March 1943.
51. AP 20/10/458, Churchill to Eden 27 Feb. 1943.
52. J. Harvey (ed.), *The War Diaries of Oliver Harvey 1941-1945* (London, 1978) p.225.
53. C. Hull, *Memoirs* (2 vols, London, 1948) vol.2, p.1213.

54. R. Sherwood, *The White House Papers of Harry L. Hopkins* (2 vols, London, 1948-1949) vol.2, p.719.
55. E. Barker, *Churchill and Eden at War* (London, 1978) p.71.
56. AP 20/10/706, Eden and Attlee to Churchill 23 May 1943.
57. AP 33/9, Churchill to Eden and Attlee 24 May 1943.
58. Kersaudy, *Churchill and De Gaulle* p.290.
59. AP 20/1/23, diary 12 and 13 July 1943.
60. Harvey, *Harvey War Diaries* p.274.
61. D. Carlton, *Anthony Eden: A Biography* (London, 1981) p.220.
62. AP 20/1/23, diary 20 July 1943.
63. AP 20/10/579, Churchill to Eden 30 July 1943.
64. Hull, *Memoirs* vol.2, p.1241.
65. K. Sainsbury, *The Turning Point* (pbk edn, Oxford, 1986) p.262; V.H. Rothwell, *Britain and the Cold War 1941-1947* (London, 1982) p.112.
66. AP 33/9, Eden to Churchill 27 Dec. 1943.
67. AP 20/1/24, diary 23 April 1944.
68. Ibid., 3 June 1944.
69. Ibid., 6 June 1944.
70. Dixon, *Double Diploma* p.92.
71. PRO, FO 954/9, Eden to Churchill 16 Jan. 1945.
72. AP 20/13/113, Eden to Churchill 7 April 1945.
73. Dilks, *Cadogan Diaries* p.496.
74. Nicolson, *Nicolson Diaries 1939-1945* p.385.
75. AP 33/9, note by Eden on Halifax to Eden 30 May 1944.
76. De Gaulle, *Complete War Memoirs* p.418.
77. AP 23/60/14A, Eden to Salisbury 28 Dec. 1957.
78. AP 23/24/32, note for biographer 1 May 1968.
79. AP 23/8/40B, Eden to Beaverbrook 18 May 1961.
80. 'I have always been troubled at the prospect of Strasbourg holding sway here. I want to work closely with Europeans in every sphere, but not to the point where we share a parliament if I can avoid it' (AP 23/26/43A, Eden to D. Donnelly 14 July 1965). Compare David Carlton's rather curious comment: 'On one issue, however, he supported Macmillan and his successors: he now accepted that Great Britain should join the European Economic Community' (Carlton, *Anthony Eden* p.476).
81. A. Eden, *Full Circle* (London, 1960) pp.36-7.
82. AP 23/64/11A, Eden to R. Turton 22 Oct. 1962.

83. D. Dutton, 'Anticipating Maastricht: The Conservative Party and Britain's First Application to Join the European Community', *Contemporary Record* 7 (1993), pp.522-40.
84. Eden endorsed de Gaulle's statement made in 1960 on the way forward for Europe. This 'must not be through dreams but in accordance with realities. Now, what are the realities of Europe? ... In sober truth, they are the states' (AP 6/3/56).
85. AP 23/17/61A, Eden to Lord Chandos 5 Oct. 1962.
86. Text in AP 26/22/245.
87. AP 23/26/17D, Donnelly to Eden 24 July 1962.
88. AP 23/24/9, note by Eden of meeting held on 29 June 1962.
89. AP 20/2/20, note in diary for 1975.
90. Eden and de Gaulle remained in touch until shortly before the latter's death. In a final letter, sent from Ireland after he had given up the French presidency, de Gaulle wrote of the 'amitié, tout à fait exceptionelle' he felt for Eden (AP 23/24/32C, De Gaulle to Eden 19 May 1969).

Film as a weapon
during the Second World War

Philip M. Taylor

The Second World War vastly increased the role and significance of film as a weapon in Britain's arsenal of 'Total War'. Like the tank and the aeroplane before it, however, this weapon needed time to become appreciated before it could be deployed to its greatest effect. Film had, of course, been used to some extent as an instrument of official propaganda and morale-boosting during the First World War.[1] Then, during the inter-war years, immense strides had been made in the area of official government publicity and documentary films by organisations such as the Empire Marketing Board and GPO Film Unit.[2] Yet in 1939, after five years of inter-departmental squabbles in the planning for propaganda in the next war, the overall place of film remained unresolved. Initially, film was considerably distrusted by those who had traditionally taken up arms for their country, with the result that Whitehall's Service Ministries at first did all they could to hinder its effective deployment. This, the Service Ministries claimed, resulted in part from the need to avoid providing the enemy with valuable information – the time-honoured justification for military censorship – but it was just as much the result of ignorance concerning the positive impact which good propaganda films could have on morale both at home and in allied and neutral countries. The protagonists of film in the Ministry of Information (MoI) considered it a key instrument of wartime propaganda, which they maintained was a 'Fourth Arm' of defence.[3] It was, however, such a different kind of weapon, attacking the heart and mind rather than the physical body, that its full potential as an auxiliary to the fighting capability of a nation at war was not immediately appreciated. Only when the options available to use other weapons, such as the Army, had been severely restricted following Dunkirk, and when the Strategic Air Offensive against Germany was fully under way, did the military mind really appreciate that potential. In short, until 1941-42 and the so-called 'end of the beginning', the Service Ministries tended to regard propaganda as 'a cheapjack charlatan game',[4] unworthy of their serious consideration.

The antipathy of military men towards the media, from the Crimean War to the Persian Gulf War, is almost carved in stone. Ever since William

Howard Russell's despatches from the Crimea to *The Times*, inaugurating not only the profession of war correspondent but also the practice of modern military censorship, the fear that the media might expose military inadequacies has lain beneath the paper-thin justification of the need to prevent valuable information from reaching the enemy and thereby to save the lives of servicemen. Once a more sophisticated attitude evolved, the media gradually came to be recruited, often unwittingly, into the process of spreading disinformation. This, however, took nearly a century to evolve. Too often the military were over-defensive about opening up their activities to the prying gaze of the media, which were felt to be ill-equipped to judge those activities in their proper context. This in turn reflected a fear of the public, whose morale was deemed to be too fickle to accommodate set-backs – although, paradoxically, this in itself reflected a growing appreciation of the increasingly important role of public accountability in the age of democracy. It is also perhaps not too fanciful to suggest that, during the early years of the Second World War, the Service Departments had themselves become victims of official British propaganda concerning the 'spy menace' and the presence of a Nazi 'fifth column' within Britain. The fear that Nazi agents might be sitting in British cinemas scrutinising newsreels for clues to troop locations and equipment appealed to the military imagination.

The impact of a single film, like that of an artillery shell or a single bomb, was not in itself likely to prove decisive. Nobody in the MoI argued that. It was, rather, the totality of the campaign which mattered. If we stretch the analogy further, and liken the different kinds of film – feature films, documentaries, official short films and newsreels – to the various branches of the armed forces, the issue becomes clearer. A coherent Grand Strategy would be required if the *cumulative* impact of the messages conveyed by different types of film were to have a more significant effect over a longer period of time, especially in a war of attrition. This would be particularly the case if the messages were reinforced by impressions made elsewhere in radio, posters, pamphlets and newspapers. It was this overall climate pervading all aspects of public life which, argued the professional propagandists, could determine the likely reception and impact of individual 'munitions of the mind'.[5] That the achievement of such a 'Propaganda State' was being sought in a democracy, even a democracy at war, raises many issues that cannot be tackled here; suffice to say that, by 1942, Britain was closer to this condition than at any time in her recent history. Yet, in order to achieve this climate of what may be termed 'Total Propaganda', considerable attention needed to be paid to each individual component, so that the sum of the parts added up to a coherent whole. In the case of the Service Ministries, this required a radical rethink of the way in which they conducted their activities, now that matters of operational security needed to be balanced alongside questions relating to publicity, information and civilian morale.

* * *

As the MoI got into its stride, courtesy of the respite provided by the Phoney War, it felt that the three fundamental axioms of British wartime propaganda should be that 'news is the shocktroops of propaganda', that it should tell 'the truth, nothing but the truth and, *as near as possible,*[6] the whole truth' and that for the 'film to be good propaganda it must also be good entertainment'.[7] These were to be the main principles on which the MoI evolved its own 'Grand Strategy' for the conduct of censorship and propaganda in a conflict which came to embrace civilian life to an unprecedented degree − a conflict in which it was felt that morale, however nebulously defined, might prove critical.

The problem lay not just with precise definitions of 'morale'. There were also debates about what actually constituted 'news' (good or bad, hot or cold, secret or public) and there was also the issue of war's often stated first casualty, the truth. Fiercely resisting the temptation to be drawn here into post-modernist theories, I shall simply say that the essential problem in 1939-40 was that the news was bad and that was the truth. This was the propagandists' nightmare. But the argument was not only that something had to be done, but that something indeed could be done to rectify the position, if only the Service Departments would give them − the propagandists − the tools so that they could finish the job.

Priority in official film propaganda at the start of the war had been given to the newsreel companies which at least had a very good track record of packaging bad news in an entertaining and even cheerful way during the Depression years. Yet this annoyed the documentary makers, who felt that their achievements in film-making during the 1930s had more of a *purpose*, especially in portraying the very working man and woman who would now be called upon to fight this war. While the 'documentary boys' fumed that they were not being similarly enlisted, their problem had been that working men and women had not, in any significant numbers, wanted to see their films; the public had wanted escapist entertainment. This was still the case at the outbreak of war when all cinemas were, very shortsightedly, closed down for a time on grounds of safety (nitrate film was highly inflammable). Yet even when they were re-opened, that champion of the British entertainment film of the 1930s, Alexander Korda, found that he had to make his first contribution to the war effort, *The Lion Has Wings* (1939), without official support (although the project did have MoI approval). It was, in any case, American feature films which the British public most wanted to see and Hollywood's record in projecting a positive, though not always realistic, image of Britain through 'historical' films such as *The Adventures of Robin Hood* (1938) and *The Sea Hawk* (1940) was second to none from a propagandist point of view. Even so, there was no way that the MoI could allow the film industry of a neutral, albeit anglophile, country to do its film propaganda work for it — although, as we shall see, they did have plans for infiltrating its films.

Despite the pioneering work of several historians,[8] much research remains to be done concerning the cumulative impact of feature films over a long period of time. Much more has been done, perhaps understandably, in the brave new world of using 'factual' film material as evidence.[9] Put at its simplest, the wartime role of official documentary films and newsreels, over which the government exercised a more immediate and direct control, was based upon an information-oriented approach to promoting certain messages at the expense of others. Any analysis of these messages can tell us much about contemporary official concerns, not just comparatively trivial ones such as 'digging for victory' or 'tittle tattle losing the battle' but also more fundamental aspects of government policy which had long-term consequences for British society as a whole: the changing role of women; the relationship between Britain and its Commonwealth; the 'accuracy of strategic bombing'; the gallantry of 'Our Soviet Friends'; wartime visions of post-war society; and possibly even the political destiny in 1945 of Winston Churchill himself.

Historians of these large issues who have looked at film sources, including Philip Bell, have learned much — not least what a rich and still relatively untapped vein of archival material such evidence provides. This is apparent from Philip Bell's work in this area in the compilation films he made with Ralph White for the Inter-University History Film Consortium.[10] Such films by historians *for* historians are designed in part to demonstrate the importance of film as an historical source. Yet it may be noted that a not dissimilar exercise was attempted by the MoI during the Second World War with a compilation film entitled *Film as a Weapon* (1941). This was never shown to a public audience but was designed to demonstrate to individuals in the Service Ministries, unconvinced of the power of the medium, what could be achieved if they extended their co-operation.

Before they examine any film as a text, historians need to be aware of its context. One of the first points to note is that the vast majority of feature films seen during the war dealt not with war themes — at least not directly — but with 'escapist' material. That said, what films do not convey is often just as significant as what they do project — an approach much loved by film scholars with their predisposition towards diegesis. However, feature films were but one course on the menu available to the cinema-going public. That public was habitually fed on a diet which also included newsreels and documentaries that were not only a principal source of information and impressions for a good many people waging Total War, but also, as I have indicated, the meat of much historical research since that time. These more 'factual' films represented in fact the harder edge of British wartime propaganda, and they can tell us much about the overall climate of the 'People's War', not just for the three hours or so it took to show them one evening, but for the six years it took to win that war. But they were, to borrow some of Nicholas Pronay's memorable phrases, 'illusions of reality' and very flawed 'windows on the world'. One needs also to remember the ever-present hand of the blue pencil censors.[11] Rarely visible, that hand was nonetheless crucial for, as Churchill once put it in a slightly different context, in effective propaganda there is no need to 'insert dots where the omissions have been made'.[12] No film exhibited publicly in Britain during the war escaped the eye of the censor; the corollary was that every film which the public saw had government approval. The scripts of feature films, for example, had to be submitted in advance of production to the British Board of Film Censorship, whereas newsreels were subjected to both pre- *and* post-censorship. Film propaganda was clearly too serious a business to be left solely to the film-makers.

Talking pictures had, of course, been in existence for a decade – but only that – before the outbreak of war. Politicians ignored the impact of film at their peril – both in the better known case of the dictatorships and also in the newly evolving democratic systems such as Britain.[13] For, during the 1930s, as A.J.P. Taylor has reminded us, going to the pictures had become an 'essential social habit' in Britain;[14] it was 'far and away the most popular entertainment', especially for the very people who had recently been enfranchised and who were now most likely to be bombed – urban working-class people and their children between the ages of 15 and 35. By 1945, 30 million people – half the population – were attending a cinema in Britain every week, a figure which had risen from 19 million in 1939. After November 1939, there were, at any given time, no fewer that 4000 cinemas in operation, showing an average of 480 mainly American feature films per year,[15] as well as a wartime total of nearly 2,000 official films produced by the MoI and over 3,000 newsreel issues. It may well be that the Second World War was a 'war of words', but for a great many people it was also a war of images, or more precisely an audio-visual war.

Many factors might have been thought to minimise the impact of the cinema: celluloid nitrate was classified as an essential war material; almost half the existing film studio space in Britain was requisitioned for war purposes, resulting in a drop in the number of operational film studios from 22 to 9; many essential personnel were called up; taxes affecting the industry were increased, with a consequential rise in seat prices; and urban cinemas were potential death-traps in bombing raids. Nevertheless, it is clear that the cinema was immensely popular, as was only too apparent to Britain's wartime morale managers. Given that almost every man, woman and child was likely to become involved in this conflict, and that, if victory came, nearly all adults would be able to demonstrate their reaction to the war's conduct at the electoral booth, the images and sounds in the cinema and the voices on the wireless in the home were likely to prove almost as vital as those which were not seen or heard as a result of the intervention of the censor.

At the top of the political command structure after 1940 was Winston Churchill — arguably British political history's greatest film fan — a man whose knowledge and enthusiasm for film was such that he instinctively recognised that his own greatest contribution would be, not through the cinema but on the radio.[16] Beneath him in the ministerial hierarchy was Brendan Bracken, one of his closest confidants, and, after July 1941, the head of the most elaborate organisation for the conduct of propaganda, censorship and political warfare which Britain had yet experienced. Unfortunately, Bracken's inheritance was such that, on his appointment, Lord Beaverbrook, who had been Britain's first Minister of Information back in 1918, felt that it would be a 'sarcastic or even an unfriendly act' to offer him his congratulations.[17] The main reason for this quip was the early wartime history of acrimonious relations between the MoI and the Service Departments.

The production of *Film as a Weapon* was in part a response to the inadequacy of British propaganda, and of film propaganda in particular, in the early stages of the war. With the MoI in chaos and still lacking that most vital of successful propaganda characteristics — consistency — as a result of four ministerial changes in its first two years of existence,[18] the lack of appropriate film material for cogent propaganda in neutral countries, and especially the USA, was a problem which demanded urgent attention.[19] The overwhelming tide of American isolationism, combined with a mistrust of foreign and especially British propaganda, created real problems, as is illustrated by a poster found in Chicago:

ABSOLUTE NEUTRALITY — NOW AND FOREVER. BEWARE THE BRITISH SERPENT. Once more a boa constrictor — 'Perfidious Albion' is crawling across the American landscape, spewing forth its unctuous lies. Its purpose is to lure this nation into the lair of war to make the world safe for international plunder. More than ever we Americans must evaluate this intruder into our Garden of Eden, appraising Britain down to the last penny weight of truth.[20]

True, the British had a colony of artists in Hollywood who, on Lord Lothian's instructions, had been told to stay where they were and work for the British war effort as a sort of fifth column, attacking the hearts and minds of the American cinema-going public via *feature* films. [21] Their importance was fully appreciated by Lothian who, in September 1939, wrote from Washington:

> It strikes me as being a great pity that the production side of the film industry should have been closed down in England ... for that means that within a short time all the films which will be shown will tend to be of American origin. It is therefore of the utmost importance that British actors, and still more British producers, who are operating in this country should be left to do so, partly because they ensure that the British point of view permeates the [film] industry, and partly because they keep alive the production of British or largely British films. [22]

As a result, directors such as Alfred Hitchcock and actors such as David Niven and Laurence Olivier, who were part of this highly secret brief, earned only public scorn in Britain for their alleged cowardice, greed and even treachery for not returning home to fight for King and Empire in their hour of greatest need, because they had supposedly 'Gone With the Wind Up'. [23] This in turn may have contributed, as the MoI believed, to the initial paucity of good feature film propaganda in Britain, as evidenced by the dreadful *The Lion Has Wings* (1939). In fact, however, the main problem was the inadequacy of suitable *newsfilm,* capable of combating the impressions disseminated by the more effectively organised German propaganda machine and, especially, the German Weekly Newsreels, the *Deutsche Wochenschau.* [24]

This might seem odd in view of the fact that, under the influence of the MoI Film Division's first head, Joseph Ball, it was initially decided that the forward thrust of British wartime film propaganda, both at home and abroad, should be through the newsreels. After all, from the early 1930s onwards, the newsreels had done a magnificent job, *inter alia*, in selling the idea of rearmament to a largely anti-war audience, while simultaneously supporting appeasement. It was the five British newsreel companies which had evolved highly professional techniques of persuasion through their editing, their use of music and their commentary, in order to provide a 'clearer' window on the complicated and chaotic world of the 1930s. Why, therefore, was it that representatives of the British Information Services in the USA and other officials abroad complained that the British were losing the film propaganda war in neutral countries?

A significant explanation is to be found in the question of access. Unlike their German counterparts working in PK (*Propaganda Kompanie*) Units, British newsreel camera-men were initially denied the kind of access to military operations which made for exciting news footage. The same, incidentally, was also true of good war photographs. Frank Darvall, deputy director of the MoI's American Division, pointed out that it was essential to maintain 'a constant supply of action photographs of real news value, of good technical quality and the kind calculated to give people the impression of the determination of the Allies and the efficiency of their Armed Forces'.[25] So preoccupied initially were the Service Departments with secrecy rather than publicity, and so steeped were they in a tradition of security which inspired a public relations philosophy of 'no news is good news', that no British newsreel camera-men were allowed to accompany the British Expeditionary Force to France; even in 1914 film crews had been permitted to do that. The footage which was taken by the army film camera-man, Harry Rignold, who had been rapidly appointed at the outbreak of war, was found to be largely unusable by the newsreel companies. These had been placed on a rota, or pool, system, which meant that they were totally dependent on official sources for film from the fighting fronts.[26] It may well be that their dismissal of footage shot by Rignold was part of a campaign to gain access to the front for themselves, which they were permitted to do, after considerable MoI pressure, in October 1939. It is equally true that, given the attitude of the Service Ministries, the pool itself was invariably dry. That attitude helps to explain the astonishing paucity of footage recording Britain's 'miracle' at Dunkirk. The only newsreel camera-man present on that occasion, Charles Martin of Pathé, did shoot a little material but was, perhaps not unnaturally, more preoccupied with helping the evacuation rather than filming it.[27]

* * *

Apart from captured enemy footage, which they had used for training and for intelligence purposes, the Service Departments had, in the early stages of the war, displayed only limited interest in film. Their interest, in other words, as Frank Capra later put it describing a similar experience in the American context, was with 'the "hows" of war, not the "whys"'.[28] Their view of film as a double-edged weapon in the context of military intelligence was probably the main reason behind their refusal to allow greater access to British camera-men; the notion of using film for positive publicity reasons was almost completely alien to them. With good reason the Royal Navy was nicknamed the 'Silent Service' and, when one bears in mind that most official censors at the start of the war were retired naval officers, and that British involvement during the first months of the war was confined mainly to naval operations, it should come as no surprise to learn that the Admiralty was the most reluctant of the service departments to furnish the MoI with news which might have a positive bearing upon morale. What is surprising is that the First Lord at that time was none other than the former war correspondent Winston Churchill, a man whose view from the official side of the fence was encapsulated in his statement that it was 'for the Admiralty or other department to purvey to the Ministry [of Information] the raw meat and vegetables and for the Ministry to cook and serve the dish to the public'. This might seem all well and good, until one realises that Admiralty offerings barely constituted famine relief to news-starved journalists. As a Minister, Churchill was no doubt deeply conscious of his experience with the media over the Dardanelles Campaign in the Great War. He began World War Two as a member of the 'no news is good news' school of thought. When, for example, Churchill refused to admit that damage had been done to HMS Nelson and HMS Barham in February 1940, Lord Lothian wrote: 'I think Winston has made a fool of himself. He is always doing these things. That is why he never becomes Prime Minister.'[29]

But Churchill was by no means alone in this attitude. At the Air Ministry, the myth of the accuracy of strategic bombing was jealously sustained in the face of curious and sceptical eyes. In September 1940 Arthur Harris was of the view that 'much mischief has already been done by giving away valuable information to the enemy at the expense of our war effort and to the lives of our crews in order to make snappy paragraphs for the gutter press'.[30] Small wonder that, in such a climate of snippets and secrecy, exaggeration of British successes became the norm, with a corresponding increase in public scepticism recorded by Mass Observation in the first half of 1940.[31] The

Navy's continuing reluctance to allow access, even during the battle of the Atlantic, was epitomised by the fact that it was left to a feature film, *In Which We Serve* (1941), starring Noel Coward, to carry the weight of public perception. This, moreover, was not until 1941. For the first fifteen months of the war, the MoI waged a running battle with the armed forces in an effort to extract stories which would cater for civilians who, having become combatants on the Home Front, had a vested interest in what was happening on other Fronts. It was this diminution of the traditional gap between soldier and civilian which called for greater mutual co-operation and understanding. Film could serve precisely this purpose in a way that no earlier medium could, and the MoI rightly felt that the Service Departments needed to be convinced of this fact.

A further – and in many ways the most critical – explanation, and one which will be considered in due course, was that British camera-men, even had they been allowed greater access, hardly had the kind of material to film which was likely to bolster morale at home and instil confidence abroad, at a time when the German war machine was blitzkrieging its way towards the English Channel. But news footage is not necessarily the same thing as factual footage; news is a managed and packaged product which is subjected to a whole host of distortions involved in selection and sequential story-telling. The facts, in other words, may have been grim, but this did not automatically mean that the news needed to be. None the less, as Churchill did recognise, in wartime actions always speak louder than words, which is why the Prime Minister was hoping that British resistance on the beaches of southern England would stir American hearts. 'If we smash the Huns here', he wrote, 'we'll need no propaganda in the United States.'[32]

Churchill soon changed his mind. For example, before too long we can find him claiming that the redoubtable character of Mrs Miniver, immortalised in the book and the 1942 film, did more for the allied cause than a flotilla of battleships.[33] The fall of France in June 1940 had been such a shock that, in the absence of opportunities to fight the enemy by more conventional means, new weapons such as propaganda began to be given greater weight. This new receptivity to propaganda was evidenced by the appointment to the MoI of people like Jack Beddington from Shell as Head of Films Division and Sidney Bernstein from Granada to organise distribution. The GPO Film Unit was transferred to the MoI in the summer of 1940 and renamed the Crown Film Unit. Here the documentary movement was at last allowed its opportunity to make film about the 'whys'. Other significant developments were the appointments of Isaiah Berlin and William Stephenson to the American propaganda organisation, the despatch to the USA of Alexander Korda, the replacement of Reith by Duff Cooper as Minister of Information, the BBC broadcast transmissions of J.B. Priestley, and the commissioning of Powell and Pressburger's *Forty Ninth Parallel* (1941) – made very much with United States opinion in mind, where it was released as *The Invaders*.[34] At the Air Ministry, matters were greatly helped by the appointment of Air Commodore Peck as head of public relations. Under him a remarkable transformation took place, to the point where the RAF earned the nickname of the 'Royal Advertising Force'.[35] His collaboration with the film-makers at the MoI's Crown Film Unit culminated in the production of *Target for Tonight* (1941).[36] As Peck recognised:

> In warfare today we cannot ... consider the release of information solely from the standpoint of absolute security. We must also take into account the maintenance of morale at home and among our allies, the maintenance of our prestige among neutral powers and the effective presentation of our case and our war effort to the world.[37]

During the Battle of Britain in the summer of 1940, the Air Ministry had seen the wisdom of granting greater access to the American press corps in London, which was centred upon Edward R. Murrow. Elsewhere, facilities for journalists, broadcasters and photographers (such as Cecil Beaton) were extended, and enormous strides were made in the improvement of documentary films such as *London Can Take It* (1940) and *Christmas Under Fire* (1941). Such developments all helped to demonstrate that positive projections could emerge from negative situations. As William Ridsdale of the Foreign Office News Department put it:

> To see British planes getting back, but only just getting back because they have been battered and riddled by the enemy, would provide the material for an impressive picture of the drain on our resources. These American correspondents would know the delicacy of such a position ... they could provide invaluable

evidence of our spirit and our needs.[38]

Yet the shortcomings of the news-based approach to British propaganda continued to be revealed in the limited access to the fighting fronts provided by the Service Departments. The newsreels, as the second most topical form of information delivery after radio, still required attention. Combat footage was the final component in the transformation that was at last under way.

If there was a single point from which this change can be traced, it was June 1940. After the fall of France, with German footage of the carefully stage-managed armistice ceremony at Compiègne widely seen around the world, it was clear to all but the most blinkered that something needed to be done about improving access for British journalists and film camera crews. The situation was summed up by one official in the following terms:

> One regrets to say that the German system of placing camera-men (and killing them off) in the front line of every advance on land, sea and in the air has produced results out of all proportion superior in dramatic quality and propaganda value to anything achieved by British camera-men. The German newsreels concentrate solely on two things — first, the overwhelming superiority of German armaments and weapons of war, and secondly, by way of contrast, on the future of their people, healthier children and the beautiful land they are to inherit. British newsreels emphasise the reverse....[39]

This was one of the reasons why the compilation film entitled *Film as a Weapon* was put together by the MoI. Using captured German footage acquired by fair means and foul,[40] a special screening was arranged at the War Office on 19 March 1941. To place further pressure on Whitehall, this was accompanied by a Beddington-Bernstein inspired press campaign in the *Evening Standard* and *Daily Express*.

Obviously, it is impossible in print to recapture the force of the film. Kay Gladstone, of the Imperial War Museum where the film is now located, has in any case published a synopsis, with stills as illustrations, which can be consulted.[41] But a resumé of the inter-titles will serve to indicate the thrust of the film's argument:

> **Caption:** The Nazis have four fighting services — Land, Air, Sea and PROPAGANDA. Propaganda has paved the way for many

German victories. Much of this propaganda was conducted by FILM. The following excerpts from German newsreels show what was made possible by their wide and purposely organised facilities. Note: For purposes of economy most of this film is shown silent.

Caption: Part One. PEACETIME. The building of a Legend. CEREMONIAL. Note: Extensive coverage and careful placing of many cameras.

Caption: Fighting Services. Remarkable cooperative facilities given by Air and Navy.

Caption: Part Two. WARTIME. The selling of German Might. 1 – The Camera with the NAVY. Showing that cameras are carried on many fighting ships.

Caption: 2 – The Camera with the LUFTWAFFE. Note: The most striking example of this was of course *The Baptism of Fire*.

Caption: The end of a dogfight. Note: Only the posting of many cameras could have secured this lucky shot.

Caption: 3 – The Camera and WAR INDUSTRIES. U-Boat Factory. Note: These scenes betray no secrets but they give confidence to the German public.

Caption: 4 – The Camera in the FRONTLINE. Invasion of Holland, Belgium and France.

Caption: 5 – The visual recording of HISTORY. The March into Paris.

Caption: The Signing of the Armistice at Compiègne. Note: This is no mere routine newsreel coverage – all was previously planned with official assistance.

End Caption: By Press, Radio and Film the legend of dictatorship was established. Press, Radio AND FILM can help our armed forces to kill that legend and reassert the message of democracy.

If there is such a thing as a single film which made a determinable propagandistic mark on its target audience, then this is almost certainly it. At its meeting on 19 May 1941, the Cabinet Defence Committee forced a more accessible approach to the media upon the Service Ministries.[42] Subsequent screenings of *Film as a Weapon* to the Air Ministry seem also to have had an impact, for in the second half of 1941 the RAF established its own Film Production Unit, while in October the hitherto under-resourced Army Film Unit was enlarged into the Army Film and Photographic Unit. These two bodies, as they grew in experience and recruited more and more people from the professional film-making community such as Captain Roy Boulting, and photographers such as Bert Hardy, produced a series of documentary images which stand as a lasting testimony to the British military effort between 1942 and 1945, complementing the record of civilian bodies such as the Fire Brigade (*Fires Were Started*). They also provided, via War Office censors and the MoI, millions of feet of film to the newsreel companies, which could at last provide a short-term indication of Britain's military achievement, as well as the kind of lasting historical record so evident in *The True Glory* (1945).[43] Such is the quality of the 'factual' film record of military activity after 1941 that it is barely recognisable when set against that which preceeded it. The improved co-operation of the War Office and Air Ministry was equally evident in the arrangements made to release personnel, actors and equipment for feature film production, thus ushering in what has been termed a 'golden age of British cinema'. In the words of Michael Powell, 'the film industry had become a war weapon'.[44]

That this was at all possible was due in no small measure to pressure exerted by the MoI prior to the appointment of Brendan Bracken as minister in July 1941, though that appointment no doubt greatly assisted the process. It helps to explain the tremendous success of *Desert Victory*, the celebrated film account of the victory at El Alamein; so successful indeed was this product that it prompted inter-service rivalry in a scramble for recognition on film of the contribution being made by the various branches of the armed forces.[45] This was so much the case that the follow-up film, *Africa Freed*, was seriously delayed. The cause was, of course, inter-service rivalry between the Army and the Air Force. The 'Silent Service' remained largely unmoved, at least until 1944, when record film of the Normandy invasion was finally taken by naval cameramen. Yet, even here, a discernible shift in attitude became apparent following proposals from Mountbatten, Chief of Combined Operations (upon whom Noel Coward based his character in the film *In Which We Serve*) and Stafford Cripps in 1942.[46]

Yet when all is said, perhaps the greatest single achievement of any

Service Department's publicity unit during the war was not the actual production of any single film or body of films. Rather, three years of propaganda concerning the Strategic Bombing Offensive resulted, in Noble Frankland's words, in 'a more or less constant concealment of the aims and implications of the campaign which was being waged'.[47] Film was used as a weapon in this concealment, rather as 'video-game' type footage was used in the Gulf War, in order to deflect attention away from what was really going on at the sharper − and inaccurate − end of conventional bombing. Given that British citizens had themselves suffered from bombing during the Blitz, the maintenance of the illusion that a *strategic* air offensive was being conducted by Bomber Command was all the more impressive. Harris, who disliked propaganda intensely and resented the use of his planes for dropping, as he put it, 'bits of bumph', was unsuccessful in his 1943 demand for a stark public statement 'that the aim is the destruction of German cities, the killing of German workers and the disruption of civilised community life throughout Germany'.[48] Instead, photographs and film footage of damage to industrial and military targets, rather than residential areas, were poured out from the Air Ministry, not just to provide a moral counterpoint to the activities of the Luftwaffe but also, until the offensive got fully under way in 1942-43, to show that Britain could not only 'Take It', she could also hit back − and that she could hit back with a high degree of accuracy, something which we now know to be patently untrue.

The improvement in British combat footage after 1941 none the less indicated a growing appreciation of the role of a newsfilm as a weapon in Total Warfare. In addition, of course, Britain was greatly helped after that date by the acquisition of propaganda-sensitive allies, who could also provide British newsreel distributors with the kind of spectacular footage supplied by Russian front-line camera-men (only too evident in the film made by Philip Bell and Ralph White, *Our Soviet Friends*) or by hardened Hollywood professionals like William Wyler, who were prepared, and indeed allowed, to accompany the 'Memphis Belle' on 1,000-bomber raids over Germany.[49] This is not to suggest that the media professionals working for the newsreel companies ceased to complain about delays in receiving timely material from the combat cameramen. The minutes of the Newsreel Association of Great Britain bear witness to this. But both the quality and the quantity of the material with which they were now being provided had improved beyond all recognition from the early days of the war. Now, moreover, there was an even more compelling reason for this improvement. For if the British contribution to the war was to be placed in its proper perspective after 1941, comparable footage of British campaigns had now become essential, as much for the popular perception in allied countries as for its effect on domestic and neutral morale – the original reason behind MoI pressure for increased access for camera-men. In other words, the *British* war effort was competing for attention alongside the American and Russian war efforts. Be that as it may, when Britain had stood alone in the war, with her back to the wall, it was perhaps just as well that her people were denied access to thrilling footage of Dunkirk or, later, of the fall of Singapore, and that they had to rely instead on the BBC transmitted oratory of Winston Churchill. Good propaganda, after all, loves a winner most of all and effective propaganda does have to be rooted in reality. Despite the success of the British in demonstrating what could be done with bad news, the probability is that if Goebbels had been able to convert Stalingrad into a Dunkirk he would have needed to do so *without* the help of film.

Notes

1. For the most recent published analysis, see the special issue of *The Historical Journal of Film, Radio and Television* [hereafter *HJFRT*] on 'Britain and the Cinema in the First World War', 13 (1993).
2. See Paul Swann, *The British Documentary Film Movement, 1926-46* (Cambridge, 1989).
3. Henry Wickham Steed, in charge of propaganda to Austria-Hungary during 1918, described in 1940 how propaganda was a 'fifth arm' behind the Navy, Army, Air Force and economic warfare: 'the weapon of the mind for the battle of wits or, on a higher level, the sword of the spirit for the war of faiths': H. Wickham Stead, *The Fifth Arm* (London, 1940). Charles Cruickshank, in his *The Fourth Arm: Psychological Warfare 1938-1945* (Oxford, 1977), used the term 'fourth arm' of attack when describing wartime psychological warfare.
4. Public Record Office [hereafter PRO], INF 1/857, Memorandum by A.P. Ryan 4 June 1941.
5. The phrase was Lord Beaverbrook's, Britain's first Minister of Information in

1918. For a general historical overview see Philip M. Taylor, *Munitions of the Mind: war propaganda from the ancient world to the nuclear age* (Wellingborough, 1990).

6. Note that it does not say 'as far as possible'. Emphasis added.

7. The respective sources for these axioms are Sir John Reith, *Into the Wind* (London, 1949) p.354, a sign displayed in the depths of the MoI offices at the Senate House, University of London, and 'Programme for Film Propaganda', 1940, PRO, INF 1/867.

8. See, in particular, the contributions in K.R.M. Short (ed.), *Feature Films as History* (London, 1981), and P. Sorlin, *The Film in History* (Oxford, 1986).

9. In particular, see A. Aldgate, *Cinema and History: British Newsreels in the Spanish Civil War* (London, 1979) and N. Pronay, 'British Newsreels in the 1930s: 1. Audiences and Producers' and '2. Their policies and Impact', in *History*, 56 (1971) pp.411-8 and 57 (1972) pp. 63-72. See also Pronay, 'The Newsmedia at War' in N. Pronay and D.W. Spring (eds.), *Propaganda, Politics and Film, 1918-45* (London, 1982).

10. 'Our Great Ally France, 1938-40', IUHFC Archive Series, No.4 and 'Images of the Soviet Union at War, 1941-45', British Universities Historical Studies in Film, No.8 (obtainable from British Universities Film and Video Council).

11. See Philip M. Taylor, 'Censorship in Britain in World War Two: an Overview', in A.C. Duke and C.A. Tamse (eds), *Too Mighty to be Free: Censorship and the Press in Britain and the Netherlands* (Zutphen, 1987).

12. PRO, PREM 3/476/3, minute by Churchill, 7 Sept. 1941.

13. T. Hollins, 'The Conservative Party and Film Propaganda between the wars', *English Historical Review,* 379 (1981), pp.359-69.

14. A.J.P. Taylor, *English History, 1914-45* (London, 1965) p.313.

15. I.C. Jarvie, *Hollywood's Overseas Campaign* (Cambridge, 1992) p.182.

16. For a discussion of Churchill's relationship with the medium of film, see D.J. Wenden and K.R.M. Short, 'Winston S. Churchill: film fan' in *HJFTR* 11 (1991), pp.197-214. By 1942, when Churchill's conversion had been achieved, he was still thinking of film as an historical record. This was his original intention for British Movietone's coverage of his first wartime meeting with Roosevelt. *Atlantic Charter* was released commercially by the MoI in October 1942. But the myth remains that Churchill was not interested in propaganda. In fact he frequently involved himself in the micro-management of its corollary, censorship, by personally stopping certain newsreel items. See, for example, Brian Bond (ed.), *Chief of Staff: the diaries of Lieutenant-General Sir Henry Pownall, Vol.2, 1940-44* (London, 1974), diary entry for 20 Oct. 1941.

17. Beaverbrook to Bracken, 21 July 1941, cited R. Cole, *Britain and the War of*

Words in Neutral Europe, 1939-45: the art of the possible (London, 1990) p.83.

18. The Ministry of Information is discussed by Ian McLaine, *Ministry of Morale: Home Front Morale and the Ministry of Information in World War II* (London, 1979) but curiously this study does not include film in its coverage.

19. For the U.S.A., see N.J. Cull, 'The British Campaign against American "Neutrality": Publicity and Propaganda,1939-41', University of Leeds PhD thesis, 1992.

20. Ibid., p.64.

21. See H. Mark Glancy, 'The Hollywood "British" Feature Film, 1939-45', University of East Anglia PhD thesis, 1993.

22. PRO, FO 371/22798, A6673, 11 Sept. 1939.

23. J.R. Taylor, *Hitch: the Life and Work of Alfred Hitchcock* (London, 1978) p.144; D. Niven, *The Moon's a Balloon* and *Bring on the Empty Horses* (London, 1983) p.160. Lothian later relented with film people of military age. See PRO, FO 371/24230, A3398/26/45, Lothian to Eden, 8 June 1940.

24. But, see K. Stamm, 'German Wartime Newsreels (Deutsche Wochenschau): the problem of "authenticity"', *HJFRT* 7 (1987), pp.239-248.

25. PRO, FO 371/22841, A8608/7052/45, Darval to Perowne, 7 Dec.1939.

26. See Ian Grant, *Cameramen at War* (Cambridge,1980) pp.8-11.

27. C. Coultass, *Images for Battle: British Film and the Second World War* (New Jersey, 1989) pp.39-40.

28. F. Capra, *The Name Above the Title: an autobiography* (London, 1972) p.329.

29. Scottish Record Office, Lothian Papers, GD40/17, Box 405.

30. PRO, AIR 14/80, Harris to HQ, 12 Sept. 1940.

31. See, for example, Mass Observation file report No.142, 27 May 1940, and PRO, INF 1/292, Home Intelligence Report No.27, week ending 9 April 1941.

32. PRO, PREM 4/25/8.

33. See Valerie Grove's introduction in Jan Struther, *Mrs Miniver* (London, 1989 reprint) p.xi.

34. The film's director, Michael Powell, recalled his meeting at the MoI when proposing the project: 'I want to make a film in Canada to scare the pants off the Americans, and bring them into the war sooner'. See his autobiography, M. Powell, *A Life in Movies* (London, 1986) pp.347ff.

35. PRO, AIR 20/2950, undated, unsigned memorandum, 'Public Relations and Censorship – Issue of communiqués and announcements'.

36. F.J. Assersohn, 'Policy and Propaganda: the presentation of the Strategic Air Offensive in the British Mass Media, 1939-45', MA thesis, University of Leeds, 1989.

37. PRO, AIR 20/2950, Peck to CAS, 28 Aug.1941.

38. PRO, FO 371/24230, A3352/26/45, Ridsdale to Monckton, 30 May 1940.
39. PRO, INF 1/568.
40. One major source for acquiring German newsreel footage was the Iberian peninsula. In Portugal, the American representative of United Artists was approached by Sidney Bernstein to supply German films surreptitiously from December 1940 onwards to the British Embassy for shipping to London and duplication. In Spain, Sir Samuel Hoare did manage to arrange an occasional exchange of Gaumont British newsreels for UFA material. See also Cole, *Britain and the War of Words*.
41. K. Gladstone, 'British Interception of German Export Newsreels and the Development of British Combat Filming, 1939-42', *Imperial War Museum Review* 2 (1987), pp.30-40.
42. PRO, CAB 147/248.
43. For the workings of Army photographers, see Jane Carmichel, 'Army Photographers in North-West Europe', *Imperial War Museum Review* 7 (1994) pp.15-22; and G. Casadio, 'Images of the war in Italy: the record made by the Army Film and Photographic Unit in Emilia Romagna, 1944-45', *Imperial War Museum Review* 4 (1989), pp.22-31.
44. Powell, *Life in Movies*, p.384.
45. Anthony Aldgate, 'Creative Tensions: *Desert Victory*, the Army Film Unit and Anglo-American Rivalry, 1943-45', in Philip M. Taylor (ed.), *Britain and the Cinema in the Second World War* (London, 1988) pp.144-67.
46. See the recommendations of the Cabinet Fighting Services Sub-committee, PRO, INF 1/860, 25 March 1943.
47. N. Frankland, *The Bomber Offensive Against Germany* (London, 1965) p.97.
48. PRO, AIR 14/843, Harris to Under Secretary of State for Air, 25 Oct. 1943.
49. The National Archives in Washington today possess 13.5 million feet of *uncut* combat film from the Second World War: Jeanine Bassinger, *The World War II Combat Film: anatomy of a genre* (New York, 1986) p.125. It is worth pointing out the difficulties encountered by the Hollywood notable, Frank Capra, in securing front-line coverage from the US Signal Corps for his *Why We Fight* 'indoctrination' films. See F. Capra, *The Name above the Title* pp.328-34, and Tony Aldgate, 'Mr. Capra Goes to War: Frank Capra, the British Army Film Unit, and Anglo-American travails in the production of "Tunisian Victory"', *HJFRT* 11 (1991), pp.24-5.

Franklin D. Roosevelt and the post-war world

Geoffrey Warner

Anyone who has worked in the Franklin D. Roosevelt Library in Hyde Park in New York cannot fail to be struck by the relatively small amount of documentation emanating from the President himself compared to the vast amount provided by others. The disparity is in large part deliberate. Roosevelt did not like committing himself to or on paper and his reluctance extended to the recording of official conversations. Thus, when the question arose in 1943 of publishing the minutes of the 'Big Four' meetings at the Versailles peace conference of 1919, not only did Roosevelt oppose publication but he also informed his Secretary of State, Cordell Hull, that 'no notes should have been kept. Four people cannot be conversationally frank with each other if somebody is taking down notes for future publication.' [1]

Such an attitude greatly facilitated Roosevelt's tendency to be all things to all people, a technique which he positively revelled in employing. As he put it to his Duchess County neighbour, friend and treasury secretary, Henry Morgenthau, in April 1942:

> You know I am a juggler, and I never let my right hand know what my left hand does ... I may have one policy for Europe and one diametrically opposite for North and South America. I may be entirely inconsistent, and furthermore I am perfectly willing to mislead and tell untruths if it will help to win the war. [2]

It would not be surprising in these circumstances if historians have sometimes misunderstood or misinterpreted Roosevelt's real beliefs and intentions. This is certainly true in the case of his foreign policy. In particular, the portrait of the president by right-wing 'revisionist' historians such as William Henry Chamberlin as a naive idealist whose failure to foresee Soviet expansionism helped set the stage for the Cold War is quite wrong. Roosevelt not only predicted the change in the balance of power after World War Two; he also had a strategy to deal with it. Opinions may differ about this strategy, and especially about whether it could have succeeded, but one thing is certain: it was based not on naive idealism, but upon hard-nosed *Realpolitik*. The purpose of this essay is to set out this Rooseveltian vision of the postwar world.

First of all, Roosevelt was well aware that an allied victory in World War Two would lead to a tremendous accretion of Russian power. This was why, despite the terms of the Atlantic Charter and the attitude of his own State Department, he took the view from the outset that the Soviet Union would hold on to the territorial gains it had made under the Nazi-Soviet pact of August 1939 and said as much to the Soviet ambassador, Maxim Litvinov, in March 1942, and to Marshal Stalin in Teheran in December 1943.[3] His chief concern was to avoid unfavourable domestic repercussions, particularly among Democratic voters whose ethnic origins were in the territories concerned. This was a particular problem in the case of the Poles. The British Prime Minister, Winston Churchill, was therefore entrusted with the disagreeable task of trying to persuade the Polish government-in-exile, which was based in London, of the need to accept an eastern frontier based on the Curzon Line of 1919, and Roosevelt coolly lied to the Polish Prime Minister, Stanislaw Mikolajczyk, on 12 June 1944, when he said that he opposed the Curzon Line, as the unfortunate Mikolajczyk discovered from the Russians and the British when he was in Moscow four months later.[4] In a conversation with the American Roman Catholic leader, Cardinal Francis Spellman, on 3 September 1943, Roosevelt even suggested that Russian influence might extend over the whole of continental Europe. 'The U.S. and Britain cannot fight the Russians', he explained, and if the worst came to the worst, he hoped 'that out of a forced friendship may soon come a real and lasting friendship. The European people will simply have to endure the Russian domination, in the hope that in ten or twenty years they will be able to live well with the Russians.'[5]

One reason why Roosevelt was prepared to tolerate this situation was because he felt that, left to its own devices, the Soviet Union would gradually evolve into a more pluralist and capitalist society. He was, in fact, one of the earliest proponents of what political scientists later came to call 'convergence', a process whereby the social systems of capitalist and socialist societies come closer together. This notion, to which Roosevelt frequently referred, was apparently first suggested to him by Maxim Litvinov, then Soviet Commissar for Foreign Affairs, during the negotiations leading to American recognition of the Soviet Union in 1933. Neither Roosevelt nor

Litvinov believed that the two systems would eventually become indistinguishable, but they did think that they would become close enough to avoid antagonism.[6]

An even more important reason why Roosevelt was relatively unconcerned about the fate of Europe was because he did not regard the continent as likely to be of particular importance in the postwar balance of power. Although his idea of the 'four policemen' (the United States, the Soviet Union, Great Britain and China) as guarantors of peace and security in the postwar world is well known, much less emphasis is placed upon his desire that, within this framework, the United States should concentrate upon the Western hemisphere and the Pacific.[7]

In order to prevent Europe from becoming a threat to world peace again, Roosevelt was fertile in suggestions for the postwar configuration of the continent. In the case of Germany he told his advisers on 5 October 1943 that he was categorically in favour of its 'partition ... into three or more states, completely sovereign but joined by a network of common services as regards postal arrangements, communications, railways, customs, perhaps power ..., etc.' These new states should be prohibited from engaging in 'all military activities, including training' and from possessing armaments industries. 'East Prussia should be detached, and all dangerous elements of the population forcibly removed.'[8] The extent to which he expected German demilitarisation to go is indicated by his statements that Germans should not be permitted to have any aircraft – 'not even a glider' – or even be allowed to learn how to fly![9] He also expressed agreement with the draconian plans of his treasury secretary, Henry Morgenthau, for the enforced de-industrialisation of Germany:[10] he only backed away from them when their leakage to the press provoked a public furore.

Although nominally an ally, General Charles de Gaulle's Free France could not expect much better treatment from President Roosevelt than Nazi Germany. The prickly general himself, Roosevelt thought, was 'owned ... body, soul and britches' by the British,[11] – a remark which would have come as a considerable surprise to the general's alleged masters in London – and he laughingly agreed with one of his advisers that de Gaulle was 'one of the biggest sons of bitches who ever straddled a pot'.[12] More seriously, as the British Foreign Secretary, Anthony Eden, wrote on 13 July 1943, 'there are grounds ... for believing that some at any rate of the governing authorities in Washington have little belief in France's future and do not wish to see France again restored as a great imperial power.'[13] The most important of these 'governing authorities' was undoubtedly the President himself. As he told Stalin at Teheran on 28 November, while Churchill

> was of the opinion that France would be very quickly reconstructed as a strong nation ... he did not personally share this view since he felt that many years of honest labour would be necessary before France would be re-established. He said the first necessity for the French, not only for the government but the people as well, was to become honest citizens.

He also said that 'he was 100% in agreement' with Stalin's view that France should not get back Indochina and that the French should pay for their collaboration with Nazi Germany.[14] In conversations with others, including the appalled Eden, Roosevelt even mooted the possibility of stripping France of some of its metropolitan territory in order to create a new state of 'Wallonia', which would also include the French-speaking parts of Belgium, Luxembourg and Alsace-Lorraine.[15]

Not all Roosevelt's schemes for the post-war re-ordering of Europe were so vindictive or unrealistic. It is easier now, perhaps, to agree with what his closest adviser, Harry Hopkins, described as 'his oft repeated opinion that the Croats and Serbs had nothing in common and that it is ridiculous to try to force two such antagonistic peoples to live together under one government'.[16] 'He opposes the resurrection of Jugoslavia', Cardinal Spellman recorded in September 1943, 'and favours an independent Croat and Slovene state.'[17] Even 'Wallonia' was conceived in part as a solution to the linguistic division which still bedevils Belgium.

If Roosevelt believed that such changes in Europe were necessary to prevent the continent from again becoming a threat to international peace and security, he was no less concerned by the situation in Asia. Indeed, the only area in which Roosevelt foresaw a possible conflict between Russian and American interests was in that continent, or to be more precise, in China. What he feared most, he told his retiring Under-Secretary of State, Sumner Welles, in September 1943,

was the flaring up of civil war in China after Japan's
defeat. The danger there was that the Soviet Union would
intervene in behalf of the Communists, and the Western
powers would be tempted or forced in their own interest to
back the anti-Communist side. We should then see ... very
much the same situation that we had witnessed in Spain
during her civil war, only on a far greater scale, and with
grave dangers inherent in it.[18]

If one consideration underlying the Yalta agreement on the Far East was the
perceived need to secure Soviet participation in the war against Japan,
another equally if not more important one was surely the desire to secure
Russian backing for Chiang Kai-shek's regime in China.

It may still appear naive that Roosevelt was so indifferent to the outflow
of Soviet power. Did he not realise that differing ideologies were only one
cause of international conflict and appreciate, like Sir Halford Mackinder and
his successors in the realm of geopolitics, that Russian control of 'the
Eurasian land mass' could not be anything other than inimical to American
interests? Given the nature of the available documentation, the answer to this
question must of necessity be tentative, but it seems likely that Roosevelt
reasoned along the following lines. In the first place, he probably felt that the
Soviet Union would be satiated, in practice if not in theory, by the expansion
he was prepared to concede. Thus, he told the Advertising War Council on
8 March 1944:

All these fears that have been expressed by a lot of people
here – with some reason – that the Russians are going to
try to dominate Europe, I personally don't think there's
anything in it. They have got a large enough 'hunk of
bread' right in Russia to keep them busy for a great many
years to come without taking on any more headaches.[19]

While Roosevelt was certainly being less than candid about his own estimate
of the likely extension of Russian power, there is no reason to doubt his
belief that the Soviet Union would face real constraints in going any further.
He knew, for example, how anxious the Russians were for American credits
to finance their post-war reconstruction. On 8 January 1945 he was informed
that the Soviet Foreign Minister, Vyacheslav Molotov, had formally

requested six billion dollars in such credits.[20] Secondly, as we have already seen, he had a strategy to prevent the Soviet Union from gaining control over China. Thirdly, Roosevelt must have realised that, however successful the Red Army might be in overrunning Europe, it posed no direct threat to the United States. To do that the Soviet Union would require a long-range bomber force and an ocean-going navy, neither of which it possessed.

Finally, if the worst came to the worst and the Russians did become a danger, Roosevelt could legitimately claim to have organised the rest of the world in such a way that they could be isolated and contained. In November 1943, for example, he approved with some minor modifications a plan from the Joint Chiefs of Staff for the acquisition of air bases in the Pacific, Latin America, the Canary and Azores islands, West Africa, Iceland, Greenland and Canada. Both Europe and the Middle East were pointedly absent from the list, which fitted in with the inclination of the Joint Chiefs of Staff – and Roosevelt himself – to avoid commitments in those regions, but as Martin Sherry has pointed out, this did not rule out a global capability. 'Implementation of the Joint Chiefs' recommendations', writes Sherry, 'would have set up a network of bases far exceeding the prewar system in both number and geographic range. From bases in the expanded network, the B-36, with an anticipated range of ten thousand miles and a target date of 1946 for completion, would be capable of striking nearly all the more populated areas of Europe and Asia.'[21]

Behind all this lay the power of the atomic bomb. Unlike some of his contemporaries, Roosevelt grasped the potential of the new weapon before it was tested. Soon after he was appointed Secretary of State in December 1944, Edward Stettinius was told about the bomb by the President. If dropped at the junction of 42nd Street and Broadway, said Roosevelt, 'the resulting explosion ... would lay New York low'.[22] And although his remark to Stalin at Yalta a few weeks later that he hoped intensive bombing would avoid the need to invade the Japanese home islands may have referred only to conventional bombing, it is likely that he also had the atomic bomb in mind.[23] Thus, after his return from Yalta, he told the Canadian Prime Minister, William Lyon Mackenzie King, who was also a party to the nuclear secret, that he believed that Japan would probably collapse three months after the defeat of Germany and that he thought the atomic bomb would be ready by August 1945.[24] He was right on both counts. Moreover, Roosevelt was determined to keep control of this devastating new weapon firmly in American hands. The most important part of the Quebec agreement between Roosevelt and Churchill on atomic energy in August 1943 was not that cooperation should continue between Britain and the Unites States, but that there should be no unilateral disclosure of information to third parties.[25]

Furthermore, the intended nature of the proposed international post-war security organisation was such that it would probably be dominated by the Unites States. At one stage, indeed, Roosevelt toyed with the idea of running the organisation himself after he had ceased to be President. In conversations in the spring of 1943 with his former ambassador to the Soviet Union, Joseph Davies, and with Mackenzie King, he likened the proposed 'four policemen' to the ruling authority of the Presbyterian church. This, in turn, would require a 'monitor' or 'moderator', in which role he clearly envisaged himself.[26] He mentioned the idea again to Morgenthau in August 1944,[27] but this was the month in which the Dumbarton Oaks conference on the United Nations Organisation began and we cannot be sure that even if Roosevelt had not died eight months later, he would have persisted in his ambition given the structure which emerged from that conference.

Even so, it is easily forgotten that until the great wave of decolonisation in the 1960s the United States could count upon a permanent majority in the United Nations General Assembly, and although the permanent members of the Security Council had a veto – which was regarded as essential by the United States as well as the Soviet Union – two of the original four could normally be relied upon to support the former. The British were always sceptical about what they regarded as Roosevelt's obsession with China, but as Hopkins recorded on 27 March 1943, 'the President feels that China, in any serious conflict with Russia, would undoubtedly line up on our side'.[28] Roosevelt's attitude towards China was also rooted in a positive appraisal of China's future. As he said on 2 January 1945, American policy was 'based on the belief that despite the temporary weakness of China and the possibility of revolutions and civil war, 450 million Chinese would someday become united and modernized and would be the most important factor in the whole Far East'.[29] Notwithstanding the postwar economic resurgence of Japan, Roosevelt's prediction does not seem nearly as far-fetched today as it did half a century ago.

In Britain's case, while the wartime alliance between it and the United States was unique in its intimacy, it was also a very unequal one. Particularly after the number of Americans under arms overtook that of Britons in 1943, there was never any doubt as to who was the senior partner. At Teheran Britain was compelled not only to accept the American timetable for a cross-channel invasion but also the appointment of an American as commander-in-chief of the operation. Later, the more or less simultaneous invasion of southern France was forced upon the reluctant British, while the Yalta agreement on the Far East was presented to them as a *fait accompli*.

Britain's increasing subordination to the United States was reinforced by the enormous financial strains to which the country had been subjected as a result of the war. On 19 August 1944 Morgenthau told Roosevelt that, on his recent visit to London, Churchill had informed him that Britain was 'broke'. 'That surprised the President', Morgenthau recorded, 'and he kept coming back to it ... He said, "This is very interesting. I had no idea Britain was broke. I will go over there and make a couple of talks and take over the British Empire."'[30] One may be forgiven for thinking that Roosevelt was only half joking. His strong, even bitter, opposition to British as well as French colonialism has been amply documented by historians like William Roger Louis and Christopher Thorne, and, as an example of his attitude, it is worth quoting the astonishing remark which Roosevelt made in July 1942 to Charles Tassig, one of his advisers on colonial affairs: 'We will have more trouble with Great Britain after the war than we are having with Germany now.'[31]

It is of course impossible to tell how Roosevelt's 'grand design' for the post-war world would have been altered if he had survived to complete his fourth presidential term in 1949. By the time of his death on 12 April 1945 changes could already be seen. In particular, he seemed to be more favourably inclined towards France. That country's liberation had shown that there was no immediate alternative to General de Gaulle and the latter's government was subsequently accorded a zone of occupation in Germany and a permanent seat on the United Nations Security Council. A month before he died Roosevelt even conceded that France might be allowed to resume control of Indochina, provided it agreed to the ultimate goal of independence.[32] Roosevelt also abandoned the notion of dismembering Germany,[33] possibly a further example of the fall-out from the row over the Morgenthau Plan, and in the event he made no attempt to prevent the re-emergence of either Jugoslavia or Belgium. No doubt other modifications would have occurred over time.

Nevertheless the basic structure remained intact. The evidence which some historians have adduced to suggest that during the last weeks of his life Roosevelt was beginning to doubt the possibility of cooperation with the Soviet Union is scant and unconvincing. On the contrary, he told his cabinet on 16 March 1945 'that the British were perfectly willing for the United States to have a war with Russia at any time and that, in his opinion, to follow the British program would be to proceed toward that end', while in his penultimate message to Churchill on the day before he died he wrote that he 'would minimize the general Soviet problem as much as possible because these problems, in one form or another, seem to arise every day and most of them straighten out'.[34]

In conclusion, it is hard not to concede that the most accurate, as well as the most concise, account of President Franklin D. Roosevelt's post-war vision is to be found in the second volume of the war memoirs of the man who, probably more than any other, stood out against it: General Charles de Gaulle. 'In his mind', wrote de Gaulle, a four-power directorate would

> regulate the problems of the world. A parliament, the United Nations, would give a democratic aspect to this power of the 'big four', but instead of leaving almost all the globe to the discretion of the other three, such an organisation implied … the installation of American power over bases spread out across all areas of the world … Roosevelt thus relied upon involving the Soviets in an entity which would contain their ambitions and in which America could marshal its clientele. Among 'the four', indeed, he knew that Chiang Kai-shek's China needed its help and that if they did not want to lose their empire, the British would have to adapt to its policy. As far as the mass of middling and small states were concerned, it was in a position to influence them by means of aid. Finally, the right of people to self-determination, the support

offered by Washington, and the existence of American bases, would bring about new states in Africa, Asia and Australasia, which would increase the number of those under an obligation to the United States.[35] This was nothing less than a recipe for United States global hegemony, and it is curious that while the Russians repeatedly accused his successors of seeking this objective, they never levelled that charge against Roosevelt. Perhaps they, too, were deceived by this twentieth-century Machiavelli.

Notes

1. Roosevelt memorandum 16 Sept. 1943, cited in *The Conferences at Washington and Quebec, 1943* (Washington, 1970) p.1338, n.4, in the series United States, Department of State, *Foreign Relations of the United States* [hereafter *FRUS:*] (Washington, 1870 et seq.).
2. Franklin Delano Roosevelt Library, Hyde Park, New York [hereafter RL], Henry Morgenthau MSS, Morgenthau Presidential diary 15 April 1942.
3. Litvinov telegram 12 March 1942, cited in Union of Soviet Socialist Republics, Ministry of Foreign Affairs, *Sovetsko-Amerikanskie Otnosheniya vo Vremya Velikoi Otechestvennoi Voini 1941-1945* (2 vols, Moscow 1984) vol.1, pp.155-6; Bohlen memorandum 1 Dec. 1943, cited in *FRUS: The Conferences at Cairo and Teheran 1943* (1961) pp.594-5.
4. Stettinius memorandum 12 June 1944, cited in the sub-series *FRUS: 1933-1945* (1950-1969), in *1944*, 3 (1965) p.1281; unsigned memorandum 13 Oct. 1944, cited in General Sikorski Historical Institute, *Documents on Polish-Soviet Relations 1939-1945* (2 vols, London, 1961-1967) vol.2 (1967) p.413.
5. Spellman memorandum 3 Sept. 1943, cited in R.J. Gannon, *The Cardinal Spellman Story* (New York, 1962) pp.223-4.
6. Roosevelt letter 12 Nov. 1942, cited in Elliot Roosevelt (ed.), *The Roosevelt Letters* (3 vols, London, 1949-1952) vol.3 (1952) p.444; Sumner Welles, *Where Are We Heading?* (New York, 1946) p.37.
7. RL, Roosevelt MSS, Unsigned memorandum 13 Nov. 1942, President's Secretary's files, box 188 (United Nations).
8. Pasvolsky memorandum 5 Oct.1943, cited in *FRUS: 1943* vol.1 (1963) p.542.
9. Library of Congress, Washington D.C. [hereafter LC], Averell Harriman MSS, box 164, Harriman memorandum 2 Sept.1943; Morgenthau MSS, Morgenthau

Presidential diary 2 Sept.1944.
10. RL, Morgenthau MSS, Morgenthau Presidential diary 9 Sept. 1944.
11. E. Roosevelt, *As He Saw It* (New York, 1946) p.74.
12. Charles E. Bohlen, *Witness to History 1929-1969* (New York, 1973) p.205.
13. Eden memorandum 13 July 1943, cited in Earl of Avon, *The Reckoning* (London, 1965) pp.397-8.
14. Bohlen memorandum 28 Nov. 1943, cited in *FRUS: The Conferences at Cairo and Teheran* p.485.
15. Avon, *Reckoning* p.373.
16. Hopkins memorandum 15 March 1943, cited in R. Sherwood, *Roosevelt and Hopkins: An Intimate History* (New York, 1950) p.711.
17. Spellman memorandum 3 Sept. 1943, cited in Gannon, *Spellman Story* p.224.
18. Sumner Welles, *Seven Major Decisions* (London,1951) p.151.
19. S.I. Rosenman (ed.), *1944-45: Victory and the Threshold of Peace* (New York, 1950) p.99, in the series S.I. Rosenman (ed.), *The Public Papers and Addresses of Franklin D. Roosevelt* (13 vols, New York, 1938-50).
20. Stettinius memorandum 8 Jan. 1945, cited in *FRUS: The Conferences at Malta and Yalta, 1945* (1955) p.312. In comparison, the United States loan to Britain in December 1945 was 3.75 billion dollars.
21. M.S. Sherry, *Preparing for the Next War: American Plans for Postwar Defense* (New Haven, 1977) p.46.
22. E.R. Stettinius, jnr, *Roosevelt and the Russians: the Yalta Conference* (New York, 1949) p.33.
23. Bohlen memorandum 8 Feb.1945, cited in *FRUS: The Conferences at Malta and Yalta* p.766.
24. University of Cambridge Library, Mackenzie King MSS, William Lyon Mackenzie King diary 9 March 1945 (on microfiche).
25. Roosevelt-Churchill agreement 19 Aug. 1943, cited in *FRUS: The Conferences at Washington and Quebec* p.1117.
26. LC, Joseph Davies MSS box 12, Davies memorandum 14 March 1943; University of Cambridge Library, Mackenzie King diary 19 May 1943.
27. RL, Morgenthau MSS, Morgenthau Presidential diary 25 Aug. 1944.
28. Hopkins memorandum 27 March 1943, cited in Sherwood, *Roosevelt and Hopkins* p.718.
29. Memorandum of 2 Jan.1945, in T.M. Campbell and G.C. Herring (eds), *The Diaries of Edward R. Stettinius Jnr., 1943-1946* (New York, 1975) p.210.
30. RL, Morgenthau MSS, Morgenthau Presidential diary 19 Aug. 1944.
31. RL, Charles Taussig MSS, Taussig memorandum 30 Nov. 1942.
32. Taussig memorandum 15 March 1945, cited in *FRUS: 1945* vol.1 (1965) p.124.

33. Roosevelt memorandum 20 Oct.1944, cited *FRUS: The Conferences at Malta and Yalta* p.159.
34. Entry for 16 March 1945 in W. Millis (ed.), *The Forrestal Diaries* (New York,1949) pp.36-7; Roosevelt telegram 11 April 1945, cited in W.F. Kimball (ed.), *Churchill and Roosevelt: The Complete Correspondence* (3 vols, Princeton, 1984) vol.3 p.630.
35. Charles de Gaulle, *Mémoires de Guerre* (3 vols, Paris, 1954-9) vol.2 (1956) pp.237-8.

Appendix

Principal publications of P.M.H. Bell

'Great Britain and the French fleet, June-July 1940', *Aberdeen University Review* 37 (1957) pp.42-56

'Note sur le blocus britannique de la France non-occupée', *Revue d'Histoire de la Deuxième Guerre Mondiale* 28 (1957) pp.91-4

'Prologue de Mers-el-Kebir', *Revue d'Histoire de la Deuxième Guerre Mondiale* 33 (1959) pp.15-36

'La guerre sur la mer à l'ouest', *Revue d'Histoire de la Deuxième Guerre Mondiale* 48 (1962) pp.65-71

'La marine britannique au combat', *Revue d'Histoire de la Deuxième Guerre Mondiale* 51 (1963) pp.41-8

'Great Britain and the rise of Germany 1932-1934', *International Relations* 2 (1964) pp.609-18

'Hitler et les origines de la seconde guerre mondiale: essai analytique', *Revue d'Histoire de la Deuxième Guerre Mondiale* 67 (1967) pp.1-12

Disestablishment in Ireland and Wales (London, 1969), vii + 397 pp.

'British policy in the Mediterranean, 1919-1939' in A. Nouschi (ed.), *La Méditerranée de 1919 à 1939* (Nice, 1969) pp.67-78

'The breakdown of the Alliance in 1940' in N. Waites (ed.), *Troubled Neighbours: Franco-British Relations in the Twentieth Century* (London, 1971) pp.200-2

'La défense de Malte, 1940-1942' in *La guerre en Méditerranée 1939-1945* (Comité d'Histoire de la Deuxième Guerre Mondiale, Paris, 1971) pp.257-80

'Hoe raakt men een mandaat kwijt? Het optreden van de Britten in Palestina tot Februari 1947', *Onze Jaren 45-70* 12 (1972) pp.366-70

'Labour pakt aan. De naoologse politiele verandering in Engeland tot 1947', *Onze Jaren 45-70* 13 (1972) pp.387-92

'Empire krimpt in. Engeland trekt zich terug uit Griekenland en Turkije (1947)', *Onze Jaren 45-70* 16 (1972) pp.483-8

A Certain Eventuality: Britain and the fall of France (Farnborough, 1974), viii + 320 pp.

'Un message, non diffusé, du général de Gaulle', *Revue d'Histoire de la Deuxième Guerre Mondiale* 107 (1977) pp.102-5

'L'ęvolution de l'opinion publique anglaise à propos de la guerre et de l'alliance avec la France, septembre 1939-mai 1940', in *Français et Britanniques dans la Drôle de Guerre* (Comité d'Histoire de la Deuxième Guerre Mondiale, Paris, 1979) pp.51-80

[with Stuart Sykes] 'Novel and history in twentieth-century France', *History* 212 (1979) pp.391-5

'War, foreign policy and public opinion: Britain and the Darlan Affair, November-December 1942', *Journal of Strategic Studies* 5 (1982) pp.393-415

The origins of the Second World War in Europe (London, 1986), x + 326 pp.

'Introduction' [with John Pinder] and 'British plans for European Union', in Walter Lipgens (ed.), *Documents on the History of European Integration* (2 vols, Berlin, 1984-1986) vol.2, pp.23-5, 156-267.

'The letters and papers of General de Gaulle', *European History Quarterly* 17 (1986) pp.486-90

[with R.T. White] 'Our great ally France, 1938-1940' [archive film with accompanying booklet] (Inter-University History Film Consortium, London, 1987)

'British public opinion and the Darlan deal', *Franco-British Studies* 7 (1989) pp.71-9.

'Censorship, propaganda and public opinion: the case of the Katyn graves, 1943', *Transactions of the Royal Historical Society* 39 (1989) pp.63-83

'Fifty years on: some recent books on the coming of the Second World War in Europe', *Historical Journal* 32 (1989) pp.739-49

John Bull and the Bear: British Public Opinion, Foreign Policy and the Soviet Union (London, 1990), iv + 214 pp.

'Shooting the rapids: British reactions to the fall of France, 1940', *Modern and Contemporary France* 42 (1990) pp.16-28

'Great Powers', *Modern History Review* 2 (1990) pp.12-15

'La Grande Bretagne, de Gaulle et les Français Libres, 1940-1944: un bienfait oublié?', *Espoir* 11 (1990) pp.27-38

[with R.T. White] 'Images of the Soviet Union at war, 1941-1945' [archive film with accompanying booklet] (Inter-University History Film Consortium, London, 1990)

'The implications of the Soviet-German pacts for Great Britain, August-September 1939', in David Wingeate Pike (ed.), *The Opening of the Second World War* (New York, 1992) pp.149-56

'Origins of the war of 1914', 'The Great War and its impact', 'Hitler's war? The origins of the Second World War in Europe', and 'Europe in the Second World War', in Paul Hayes (ed.), *Themes in Modern European History 1890-1945* (London, 1992) pp.106-38, 129-51, 227-48, 249-73

'Grossbritannien und die Schlacht von Stalingrad' in Jürgens Förster (ed.), *Stalingrad: Ereignis − Wirkung − Symbol* (Munich/Zurich, 1992) pp.350-72

'Some French diplomats and the British c.1940-1955', *Franco-British Studies* 14 (1992) pp.43-51

[with P. Morris] 'Les "Europe" des Européens ou la Nation d'Europe', in R. Girault (ed.), *Europe des Européens* (Paris, 1993) pp.67-76

'Les attitudes de la Grande Bretagne envers l'Europe et l'integration Européenne, 1940-1957', *Revue d'Histoire Diplomatique* 108 (1994) 113-27

INDEX